Detroit Studies in Music Bibliography

Editor
J. Bunker Clark
University of Kansas

ARNOLD SCHOENBERG
France, 1933

From Arnold Schoenberg's Literary Legacy:

A Catalog of Neglected Items

by

Jean and Jesper Christensen

DETROIT STUDIES IN MUSIC BIBLIOGRAPHY   *NUMBER 59*
HARMONIE PARK PRESS   *1988*

Photographs.
Courtesy Arnold Schoenberg Institute

Printed and bound in the United States of America
Published by
Harmonie Park Press (*formerly* Information Coordinators)
23630 Pinewood
Warren, Michigan 48091

Editor, J. Bunker Clark
Art Director, Nicholas Jakubiak
Typographer, Elaine Gorzelski

Library of Congress Cataloging in Publication Data

Christensen, Jean, 1940-
    From Arnold Schoenberg's literary legacy : a catalog of neglected
items / by Jean and Jesper Christensen.
        p.   cm. — (Detroit studies in music bibliography: no. 59)
    Includes bibliographies and indexes.
    ISBN 0-89990-036-4
    1. Schoenberg, Arnold, 1874-1951 — Manuscripts — Catalogs.
2. Schoenberg, Arnold, 1874-1951 — Written works — Bibliography —
Catalogs.   3. Arnold Schoenberg Institute — Catalogs.
I. Christensen, Jesper, 1941-   .   II. Title.   III. Series: Detroit
studies in music bibliography : 59.
ML134.S33C5 1987
016.78′092′4 — dc19   87-29627

To the Memory

of

Clara Steuermann

Contents

Appendixes

Preface

In 1979 a research assistance grant from the Sinfonia Foundation provided funds for a project at the Arnold Schoenberg Institute in Los Angeles. The original proposal was defined as an archival analysis of essentially unidentified and previously uncataloged materials in the legacy. The project eventually was to include some two hundred items which numbered about six hundred pages of autograph and printed materials.

Circumstances determined the selection of papers for consideration. After Schoenberg's death many persons were privileged to cull the composer's collection of writings in search of items of specific interest. As these were set aside, the arrangement determined by the composer was progressively disturbed. When the Archive was established in 1974, all such pieces received particular designations within the retrieval system that finally retained little vestige of Schoenberg's own system of organization. Thus a rather large and widely diversified group of materials remained essentially unaccounted for. These items were frequently the less coherent products of the composer's pen: many were fragmentary or rough drafts of large, mostly incomplete, projects with blurred or shadowy profiles.

Careful analytic attention was needed to identify these pieces and to place them in proper relationship to the better-known items in the collection. As finding time for such a task in the course of the busy daily schedule of the Archive was problematic, the archivist, Clara Steuermann, designated this group of materials as a proper objective for the research time provided by the grant. The present catalog represents the final stage of that project; it describes in full two large sub-groups of Schoenberg's manuscript collection, and substantial portions of several others. It will thus facilitate access to information which has been generally inaccessible or which has received little attention until now. Care has been taken to treat the items comprehensively, so that while the present catalog complements and supplements existing catalogs and on-going descriptions of the materials in the legacy, it is also the first stage of an effort eventually to create a comprehensive and complete listing of the entire collection. Such a project, which is admittedly ambitious, can best be accomplished in stages.

A significant number of pieces in the present group are of exceptional interest, and the date of Schoenberg's earliest extant manuscripts has been more definitively established. But perhaps the most interesting aspect of the project was the restitution of Schoenberg's own systematic ordering of his literary materials and the revelations concerning his relationship with his own work.

The work in this volume owes a good deal to many persons. The support of the Sinfonia Foundation served to initiate the study and to provide a period of time during which the authors achieved an in-depth orientation to the material. This was fortunate, for thereafter circumstances dictated that all ensuing work on the project be carried out from long distance. We would particularly like to thank Jerry McBride, then acting archivist at the Institute, who stepped in when he was needed; without his courteous and knowledgeable response to all our questions and requests we would have foundered. We are especially indebted to his meticulous corrections of the final draft. Thanks are also due to Karl-Werner Guempel for a very careful reading of the final text. To Paul A. Pisk we are deeply grateful for his unflagging interest in the project; his keen appetite for knowledge was a source of sustained encouragement. We want to thank especially Lawrence Schoenberg and the Schoenberg family, whose model generosity is one of our most valued resources and whose idealism continues to benefit all students and scholars interested in the thought and music of Arnold Schoenberg. For permission to quote from the sources we are grateful to Lawrence Schoenberg and to the Arnold Schoenberg Institute.

We would like to dedicate this volume to the memory of the Institute's first archivist, Clara Steuermann, who so generously shared with us her knowledge and admiration for the treasure with which she was entrusted.

JEAN CHRISTENSEN
University of Louisville

JESPER CHRISTENSEN

September 1987

PART I INTRODUCTION

Arnold Schoenberg

and

His Literary Manuscripts

An understanding of Arnold Schoenberg's literary legacy is essential to any study of Schoenberg the composer, the theorist, and artist. First-hand acquaintance with the materials reveals that his literary manuscripts were both a repository and a resource for his creative thought. His papers embodied his faith in himself and he took care to preserve them intact through even the most difficult periods of his life which included extended periods away from his native city and finally the enforced uprooting of his physical existence when he emigrated to America. The collection represented in this catalog, which spans all phases of the composer's development, provides a rich source for the portrait of a person whose creative intellect never rested.

For Arnold Schoenberg, his writings were no less significant than his work in other forms. Like the musical scores, theory texts, and paintings, his varied literary endeavors are manifestations of his search for the spiritual essence in things and for ultimate truth. They are not merely circumstantial evidence of the composer's urge to express himself, nor are they incoherent notes and commentaries. He signed and dated most items — even marginal glosses or later additions — and created a cross-reference system with which he could keep track of his interrelated concerns, thoughts, and preoccupations.

In the present collection are papers from the late 19th century to the final years of the composer's life. They include long and short essays, aphorisms, sets of drafts, notebooks, and "concept" papers in various states of preservation. Frequently he devised bindings and covers for the items. For instance, sometimes he took something as simple as a piece of brown paper, folded or stapled it around the manuscript, indicated his own categorical designation on the front, and perhaps pasted a title or table of contents to the front side. At other times the bindings were more elaborate. For example, sometime in the 1940s at his residence in Brentwood, he made several small oblong notebooks with black cloth bindings. The leaves are prepared so that blank pages alternate with pages on which music staves are drawn in ink. In addition to organizing the materials, the cover, whether simple or elaborate, also protected the papers. Thus an essay written in pencil on poor quality paper long ago can still be read.

In 1932, Schoenberg made the first major effort to bring order to his personal papers. He was then in his late fifties and had been a prolific writer for decades. His collection of writings was large, but only a portion had been published. His decision to review all his papers at that time apparently was inspired by the political climate in Berlin—more conducive to the work of organizing a large number of unruly papers than to working on more creative projects. During his residence in Spain immediately preceding, he had already expressed his unhappiness at the thought of going "back to Berlin among the swastika-swaggerers and pogromists."[1] Upon his return (2 June 1932), he spent much of his time putting things in order:

> But although there are days when I am intensely busy sifting, sorting, and filing the "little manuscripts" I've been piling up for some 15 years and collecting the printed essays and also my lectures, there are often several days at a time when I don't feel like sitting down at my desk to do anything that requires concentration. The times aren't such that one can always keep one's mind on one's work and let one's thoughts run freely.[2]

In a letter to Berg he indicated something of the dimensions of the project and mentioned one of his goals:

> Recently I began sorting out and arranging my "literary works" (finished and unfinished). At a rough estimate they amount to 1,500 pages of print—more if anything! that makes 4-5 pretty thick books—apart from the *Harmonielehre* and the volume already published [*Texte,* 1926]. I intend publishing some of it now — (much only after my death, and other people's) — but it's probably going to be difficult, these days, to find a publisher who has enough money (to put into this commercially sound proposition).[3]

The hoped-for publication did not materialize until nearly 20 years later when *Style and Idea,* the volume of essays in English translation, appeared in America.

$$*\qquad\qquad*\qquad\qquad*$$

Schoenberg's endeavor in 1932 went far beyond the simple task of scanning the manuscript pages for possible items to publish. His extant lists of papers from this period, as well as those from later years, are evidence of his sustained commitment to order and coherence. He thoroughly revised his manuscripts and arranged them proceeding in a manner comparable to one used in establishing an archival reference system. He placed the items in roughly chronological order, stamped each with a number, and entered it on a list

---

[1] Schoenberg to Joseph Asch, dated Barcelona, 24 May 1932, in *Letters,* p. 164.

[2] Schoenberg to Anton Webern, dated Berlin, 12 August 1932, in *Letters,* p. 166.

[3] Schoenberg to Alban Berg, from Berlin, 23 (and 26) September 1932, *Letters,* pp. 167-68.

with a brief indication of contents, the number of pages, the date of origin, and his own designation which indicated its place in the collection. As he entered the designation on the list, he also wrote it on the manuscript itself. His list, or log, created at this time is in the form of a small notebook in the Institute's Archive. An interesting document in itself, it is hand-made from graph paper: three double sheets are folded and sewn together, making a total of 12 pages. Each page is divided into double columns for the entries, which comprise a number, a designation, the title of the piece, and a date. Entries for items 1 to 350 are found on pages 1 to 9. These are handwritten in ink with some additional notes in various colored pencils; each number corresponds to the stamped one on the relevant manuscript. With the exception of no. 350, dated 1938, all of these pieces are dated 1932 or earlier. This early "List of Manuscripts" was extended later by a typewritten one with an additional 77 items (nos. 351-426), most of which dated in the 1930s. The last entry, exceptionally a handwritten one (no. 427), is dated 1940.

The later typed portion of the list comprises four pages, each divided into four columns with the following headings: "No.," "Title," "Folder" (that is, the category), and "Date." In the later entries Schoenberg usually followed American dating practice with the month preceding the day and year. When he reverted to European dating style, he often used a Roman numeral for the month. The numbers are typed, not stamped as before; the corresponding items in the collection are marked with numbers and designations in black crayon pencil. The two parts of Schoenberg's list are transcribed in Appendix II of the present catalog. It is referred to hereafter as "Manuscript List A."

The classification system begun in 1932 generated a number of subcollections in addition to the large one cataloged under "manuscripts." Schoenberg produced a list for each of these collections. Thus, "Gedruckte Artikel, Aphorismen, etc." [sic] dated "Juli - 1932," is a separate list for his published articles.[4] Though he did include drafts, proof-sheets, and copies of his articles under "manuscripts," only exceptionally did he include published versions. As it was part of the comprehensive task Schoenberg undertook in 1932, the list itself was noted on the composer's manuscript list, but without a number—that is, between items numbered 251 and 252. His major poetic or creative writings were gathered together under the general category DICH[TUNGEN]. The list for this collection contains 33 items.

Apparently successful in establishing control of his papers in 1932, Schoenberg was able to transport them through the events of the succeeding years, which included the dismissal from his position at the Academy of the Arts in Berlin and his journey of exile via Paris to America where he found a home at last in Brentwood, California, in 1936. Sometime after 1940, Schoenberg returned to his collection and his earlier classifications of 1932. On a new list largely devoted to writings from the 1930s, he now included a number of older manuscripts that had been excluded from the earlier one. Of special interest are several very early writings, quite possibly the earliest

---

4 See facsimile in Walter B. Bailey, "Schoenberg's Published Articles: A List of Titles, Sources, and Translations," *Journal of the Arnold Schoenberg Institute* 4, no. 2 (November 1980): 158-59.

extant manuscripts from Schoenberg's hand. Judging from the content, they clearly originated in the last decade of the 19th century, and thus establish more precisely than before the date of the earliest manuscripts.[5] Several of these pieces are found in the present catalog under the designations KLEINE MANUSKRIPTE and FRAGMENTE, two new categories he created in the 1940s. The new list, titled "List of Manuscripts of articles, essays, sketches, etc.," consists of a typed portion (nos. 1-113) with items dated no later than 1940, and a handwritten portion (nos. 114-139) in several different hands, among them Schoenberg's. The dated articles originated between 1948 and 1951. It is referred to as "Manuscript List B," and is transcribed in Appendix III.

*   *   *

Schoenberg defined very well the boundaries of his intellectual world in the designations he originally devised for his collection in 1932. An annotated list of the terms Schoenberg used in preparing Manuscript List A is found on the pages of a notebook devoted entirely to the task of organizing the writings.[6] The composer indicated on two of the pages the types of manuscripts to be included in the individual categories.[7] Considering the huge body of writings on a wide variety of subjects written over a number of decades, it is surprising how well these categories fit the subjects and ideas.

In addition, Schoenberg devoted some four pages in the notebook to an unfinished attempt to make an alphabetical list of titles (or incipits in some cases) of all his articles. Finally, the notebook also contains 10 pages prepared so that each one corresponds to one of 10 categories for the purpose of listing all items according to its assignation. The eleventh category devised at the time, MORAL, was overlooked for some reason. Each of these 10 sheets was to have a hand-made tab with its heading attached to the upper edge of the page. Schoenberg never completed this phase of the organization, but he prepared folio-sized folders, each marked with the designation of one specific category.

Not all 11 categories designated for Manuscript List A proved useful. ANEKDOTEN and NATUR hardly materialized, and after 1933 Schoenberg added another, JEW, to provide a place for his writings on Jewish affairs.

---

5 Schoenberg dates the piece "Das Opern und Concertpublikum und seine Führer," FRAGMENTE I, 5, with the indirect reference "Die Literatur und die Malerei haben im letzten Viertel dieses Jahrhunderts [i.e., 1875-1900] merkwürdige Wandlungen durchgemacht." In FRAGMENTE I, 8, the composer refers to a certain singing teacher in Vienna, Gärtner, with whom he was associated in 1898, according to Stuckenschmidt, *Schoenberg,* p. 37. The draft for the tone poem "Hans im Glück," FRAGMENTE I, 6, has been dated by Maegaard, *Studien* I, p. 31, together with the sketches for *Gurre-Lieder,* ca. 1900.

6 The notebook is presently in a folder labeled "Notes and Indexes." It is undated, but details of the contents serve to place the origin in 1932: "Vormerkungen" refer to persons with whom Schoenberg was in contact in 1932; the writing on one of its pages is found on the Manuscript List A, no. 271, dated 1932; and another page in the book has a draft for one of the items in the present catalog, BIO III, 32, which is dated "12.XI.1932."

7 These pages have been transcribed in Appendix I; those published previously in Rufer, *Works,* p. 152, and Vojtech, *Schriften,* p. x, fail to render correctly the characteristic features of the document.

MUSIKALISCHES is the biggest group and contains more items than any other; it accounts for about one-third of all entries. Manuscripts from this group have received the most attention from commentators and have been the most extensively studied and published of the entire legacy. Consequently, only a few of these items are found in the present catalog.

The classification scheme emerged from the discrete areas of Schoenberg's thought and concerns. When an idea or subject of one paper related to more than one area of interest, he made copies of those items, or of pertinent segments, and placed them accordingly. On these occasions he indicated the cross reference on the manuscripts themselves. In some instances he compiled and revised older items and assembled like materials together in one group. For example, between September and November of 1932 the composer compiled a set of aphorisms which he copied from earlier drafts. These "Abschriften" comprise APHORISMEN I, 49.

As part of his inclination to polish, revise, or amend, Schoenberg often added commentary, glosses, and additional material during his periods of organizing activity. He usually also provided headings or titles. Later notes on earlier pieces sometimes provide unexpected insight into the composer's thought. He occasionally modified his earlier statements. For instance, in BIO III, 13, he noted his decision to change a possibly offensive remark about Richard Strauss in an earlier article. In BIO III, 39, he reviewed his friends, and in BIO III, 30, he reevaluated his enemies. In "PEACE," from 20/VIII. 1932, he wrote the following:

> In these pages one finds many statements which are extremely vehement. After even a short time, I would not have been able to justify a lot of them, and today doing that would be still more difficult. . . .
>
> This is not to say that I think differently about the injustice that was done.
>
> However, now I have realized one thing: how easy it is to be unjust oneself —
>
> And yet not be evil. [BIO III, 2][8]

*   *   *

The order of the collection devised in 1932 was gradually disturbed. Schoenberg himself made changes when he worked on it in the early 1940s. In the late 1940s many items were selected for possible inclusion in the first collection of Schoenberg's essays, *Style and Idea,* published in 1950. After

---

[8]   *Ruhe*

In diesen Blättern befindet sich manche Äusserung, die von grosser Heftigkeit ist. Sehr viel davon hätte ich schon kurze Zeit darauf nicht mehr verantworten können, weit weniger aber kann ich das heute. . . .

Damit soll nicht gesagt sein, dass ich über das Unrecht anders denke.

Nur weiss ich heute noch besser: wie leicht man selbst Unrecht tut — und doch nicht schlecht ist.

Arnold Schönberg

Schoenberg's death many persons searched for items of interest. Josef Rufer's classifications in his comprehensive catalog of 1957 deviate somewhat from those on Schoenberg's lists. It is now unclear to what extent Rufer's lists reflect the actual order of the manuscripts at that time. He states in his general description that he followed the composer's order as closely as possible,[9] and it seems that what he achieved was a reconciliation between what he actually found and what Schoenberg's lists indicated. It has been assumed that the letters "A - L," which Rufer used to designate classes of manuscripts, are his own and that he might have written them on some of the items himself.[10] Later many items were disbound and shifted during a project to microfilm the legacy.

The final stage in this process occurred when the Archive at the Arnold Schoenberg Institute was established in 1974-76. The archivist, Clara Steuermann, decided to preserve the ideas rather than the artifacts as her governing principle, and consequently separated all remaining bindings, folders and pages, and began the process of identifying and designating each piece in the collection.

However, the vestiges of the composer's own order is preserved in the designations on the manuscripts themselves and on his lists. As the material represented in the present catalog was analyzed, the system of organization, together with evidence from the revisions, gradually became clear. It is, as several writers have commented, patently impossible to reestablish any of the various orders in the legacy in use during the composer's lifetime. The reason is obvious: the collection constitutes a vital and responsive repository of his ideas, and his own later attempts to reorganize were subject to considerations of time and practicality. His persistent activity as a writer resulted in an ever-increasing volume of items requiring some control in order to be useful. As his later efforts at reevaluation and reorganization were never as thorough as that of 1932, we have problems with the chronological ordering, conflicting sets of numbers, and irregular patterns of duplication. However, all these difficulties do not minimize the importance of understanding Schoenberg's original system.[11] Other later intentions did not change the value nor alter the scope of what he had done in the earlier years, and his later alterations left a record of the evolution of his ideas.

*　　　　　*　　　　　*

The present collection of materials offers a broad range of new and revised information about Schoenberg. Together with the opportunity afforded by

---

[9] *Works,* p. 18.

[10] Cf., KL. MANUSCRIPTE I, "C-29," APH V, "C-85," APH IV, "C-83," in which the "C-" numbers have been written on top of the numbers "29," "83," and "85," which might be Schoenberg's own.

[11] See Christensen, "The Spiritual and the Material in Schoenberg's Thinking," *Music and Letters* 65, no. 4 (October 1984): 337-44.

access to an increased number of items, there is the advantage of having items which belong together, but which had been scattered, reassembled into coherent units. It is interesting to contemplate all the parts — once separated, now re-united — of Schoenberg's practical joke on future music historians — his *vexier etui* with its English translation of the German text, and the little hand-made puzzle. Equally interesting, though very different, is the reassembled orchestration text with its outline, numerous musical examples, and draft letter to composers requesting permission to quote segments of their work.

The representation of the composer's subcollections BIOGRAPHISCHES and APHORISMEN is complete here. All items designated by Schoenberg for either category have been listed and described. Thus, the printed documents for the biographical dictionaries are found together with the composer's plan for his autobiography, the usual assortment of generations of professional résumés accumulated over a period of some decades, a medical résumé, and numerous essays and commentaries detailing the composer's relationship to the rest of the world.

One of the most rewarding finds of the study is the cluster of materials related to Schoenberg's planned autobiography which was to be of a character-istically unique design. Aside from its intrinsic interest and value, the project offers a clue to much in the BIOGRAPHISCHES category where we find perpetual assessment of all statements and attitudes — his own and others he encountered. He placed his faith in a hidden order behind the apparent confusion of perceptible events, an order that might be grasped by means of artistic intuition. He believed that a truthful record of his life and thoughts would emerge from a process which he describes in his first plan for the autobiography from 1924:

> I have for a long time been planning to write my autobiography in such a way that I, to the best of my memory, will present all persons with whom I have been in contact, in so far as their relationship to me is of some interest; I will describe them as they have shown themselves to me and characterize the relationship between them and me. Of course, this is not primarily an act of revenge; rather it is merely a system which I expect will help my memory. As I proceed, the links between different persons and separate events should emerge, and I thus should be able to be as truthful as possible; while I surely would fail if I attempted to write a chronological representation. . . . [BIO III, 7][12]

---

[12] Ich plane seit langem, eine Geschichte meines Lebens zu schreiben, welche dadurch zustande kommen soll, dass ich[,] soweit mein Gedächtnis es zulässt, alle Menschen, mit denen ich in Berührung gekommen bin, soweit sie und ihr Verhältnis zu mir interessant sind, so darstelle, wie [sie] sich mir gezeigt haben und genau erzähle[,] in welchen Beziehungen wir zu einander gestanden sind. Natürlich ist das nicht in erster Linie ein Racheakt, sondern soll wirklich bloss ein System sein, von welchem ich mir verspreche, dass es mein Gedächtnis erschliessen wird. Es werden sich von Person zu Person die Glieder finden und die Ereignisse[,] und so glaube ich wirklich so wahrhaftig zu werden, als es nur irgend möglich ist; während der Versuch einer chronologischen Darstellung mir unbedingt misslingen dürfte. . . .

In July 1932, he added a title, "Biography in Confrontations,"[13] to the above concept and drafted an outline in which he listed only the important transitions in his intellectual development:

How I became a Musician
How I became a Christian
How I became a Brahmsian
How I became a Wagnerian [BIO II, 1][14]

The subject matter was to be the exchange of ideas, the perpetual renewal of thought, documented in his collection of papers.

Several aspects of Schoenberg's creative personality become especially clear when studied in relation to the collection of catalog materials, particularly those of his preferred literary style and his playful side exemplified in the aphorisms which were naturally Schoenberg's most congenial literary genre. Terse commentaries, epigrammatic and paradoxical with implied and second meanings, were the composer's means of achieving the clear uncompromised expression that was his goal. He wrote aphorisms throughout his career, and periodically he produced long sequences of them. Schoenberg's concept of what constituted an aphorism was liberal. While most are short and terse, a number of them are equivalent to short essays. They are frequently witty, sharp, and biting. Aphoristic expression pervaded his writing. Many statements in his essays are aphoristic, and many of them are expanded aphorisms. Observations easily became aphorisms and they in turn easily became commentaries, essays, or poetry. The great number of aphorisms recorded in the present work enhances our understanding of Schoenberg's literary style and working procedure. In his large-scale writings the complex forms are frequently generated by means of short concentrated formulations of distinct ideas.[15] Thus, even though all items marked "Aph[orismen]" are included here, it will never be really possible to make an exhaustive compilation of every aphorism Schoenberg wrote.

This catalog supplements the known image of Schoenberg, particularly as an author. It highlights the coherence of the composer's thought on all levels of his various activities and concerns, and it confirms our impressions of the consistency of his verdicts, beliefs, and expressions. He once wrote, "Everything I have written has a certain inner likeness to myself."[16] In this mixed assortment it is perhaps more obviously true than in any other possible selection of his writings.

---

13 "Lebensgeschichte in Begegnungen"

14 Wie ich Musiker wurde
Wie ich Christ wurde
Wie ich Brahmsianer wurde
Wie ich Wagnerianer wurde

15 See the description of Schoenberg's literary process in Jean Christensen, "Arnold Schoenberg's Oratorio *Die Jakobsleiter*" (Ph.D. dissertation, University of California, Los Angeles, 1979), and Pamela C. White, "The Genesis of *Moses und Aron*," *Journal of the Arnold Schoenberg Institute* 6, no. 1 (June 1982): 8-55.

16 *Letters*, p. 143.

Guide to the Catalog

Each entry in the catalog has three parts: the catalog designation, an analytic or descriptive commentary on the contents of each item, and a description of the item. It is germane to mention here the authors' policy with respect to the inconsistencies of spelling and grammar in the texts, much of which was the result of Schoenberg's haste in making his notations, or due to his tendency to add details to earlier items, as well as to the personal nature of the pieces. Designated mostly for his own use, these texts were rarely proofread or corrected; this is true particularly of his lists of papers which he used for his own reference.

Thus, in the writing which sometimes use idiosyncratic grammar, or simply old-fashioned (perhaps specifically Viennese) grammar, we find also frequent omission of commas (see for instance, BIOGRAPHISCHES III, 7, quoted in note 12, above), and of periods following particular abbreviations (for instance, "etc"). He might also skip apostrophes in word contractions (for instance, "habs" for "hab's," in KLEINE MANUSKRIPTE I, 14, or "lernts" in KLEINE MANUSKRIPTE II, 2). He omitted hyphens in compound nouns ("Anti Kritik," Appendix II, #162, or "Zwölfton Komposition" in APHORISMEN I, 26c, with other examples in NOTEBOOKS II, s; Appendix II, #49, #383, #426; Appendix III, #131). In the above instances, the deviations from normal procedure have been noted with square brackets or with *sic*.

However, in other instances, some of which might actually be considered more matters of personal preference, the original formulation has been retained with no further comment. These include Schoenberg's occasional insertion of an "s" between two parts of a compound word (for instance, "Militärszeit," APHORISMEN I, 24d), or the capitalization of an adjective in a title (for instance, see Appendix III, #12, #109). In his earliest writings he frequently chose "Ue," "Ae," and "Oe," for Ü, Ä, or Ö, respectively. This habit was naturally enforced by his emigration when he chose to anglicize his name (never thereafter using the umlaut form) and when typewriters with the necessary keys became a rarity. Another particular trait also apparently inspired by his emigration was his use in German texts of the English apostrophe before a genitive "s" (see KLEINE MANUSKRIPTE I, II, III, covers). In one inexplicable instance,

Schoenberg even inserted one into a German text that predates his emigration (see APHORISMEN I, 20.1).

Catalog Designation

Generally the classifications in the catalog are Schoenberg's own, noted on the items themselves by the composer. Three of these appear on his "List of Manuscripts," which served as a kind of shelf list for his collection.

It is necessary to note that three of the classifications used in the catalog are not Schoenberg's own. Two of them, JENS QUER and NOTEBOOKS, were devised to designate items that had common characteristics in each group. The first collects all items which pertain to the character Jens Quer, created in the early 1920s, who was, in effect, Schoenberg's alter ego. Schoenberg marked most of these items with this name and may have at one time considered them as a group. Several of them, however, are designated with another category, MUSIKALISCHES, which is otherwise not represented in the catalog. The collection of small notebooks includes, as a centerpiece, three rather elegant volumes made by Schoenberg himself. The rest were purchased. The contents of all notebooks here are miscellaneous in character and as such they adhere to no other particular group. Finally a third designation, MISCELLANEOUS, was used for the items with no distinguishing characteristics by which they could be associated with other items elsewhere in the collection.

With respect to Schoenberg's own categories, special note should be made that BIOGRAPHISCHES III contains all the items marked by the composer with the designation "Biographisches" (or, more commonly, "Bio") and follows the basically chronological sequence in which they appear on the composer's "Manuscript List" (designated in this catalog as Ms. List A). The items not on that list were placed elsewhere in the BIOGRAPHISCHES classification according to content and chronology. APHORISMEN I similarly contains all items marked by the composer with his own designation "Aph"; here too, the order found on Schoenberg's list is followed.

Roman numerals indicate main subdivisions within groups and reflect a natural sub-grouping of subject matter. Whenever possible the general order of presentation is chronological. The individual items are numbered with Arabic numbers; the italicized designations and numbers found in the same column are Schoenberg's own. They are included for further reference and with the purpose of demonstrating as much as possible the composer's own order or sequence.

Individual items are numbered separately, even in those instances where they were once, or perhaps are still, bound together in some manner. Copies made by mechanical reproduction (carbon, photocopy, print, and film copies), as well as handwritten ones, are found throughout the collection. These duplicates are given the same Arabic number as the original, followed by a period and a second number; hence, "1.1" and "1.2" indicate an item and a copy of that item, respectively. Individual items found in a series, such as the collection of aphorisms found in a uniform arrangement on one or more pages, are identified by the number of the collection with lower case letters in alphabetic series as needed: "16," "16a," "16b," etc., indicate first the collection and then the individual items in the collection in order of appearance. Disbound covers are given individual numbers only if they contain writing of special interest — such as a table of contents — in addition to the title, date, and/or designation. Otherwise they are identified with the special designation "Cover," and the same number as the item with which they are associated.

Title, when present, and incipits head each subject entry, followed by a description or analysis of the contents. In this description a distinction is made between published and unpublished items. The former are described only in broad terms, the latter in some detail. References for locating the publication of the items in the original and in translation are provided wherever possible. Published aphorisms are represented only by incipits. Cross references to related, or to pertinent, items are in square brackets. **Subject**

Information about the physical appearance, the bibliographic identity, and the location and date of origin of each item is in that order. Distinction is made between handwritten, typed, or printed items, and betweeen the following types of materials: manuscript, note, article, notebook, letter, and document. The term manuscript ("Ms."), whether handwritten or typed, indicates here a creative piece of writing and one which contains independent thought, however sketchy and brief it might be. A note ("N.") indicates the recording of detail or fact and contains essentially no independent thought. In this way, aphorisms, many of which are very short and terse, are termed "manuscripts," while some commentaries which might be considerably longer are identified as "notes." Making this distinction was often problematic, and it is hoped that when there is some doubt the commentary will clarify the issue. **Bibliographic Description**

The number of pages is determined by noting the presence of writing on a side; thus, a sheet with writing on both sides is "2 pages." In the case of the notebooks, a count of the total number of pages is given in the general description of the item, and the number of pages (or sides) involved in each separate entry in the book is given also.

Provenance and dates on the items themselves are provided in italics. Schoenberg's varied dating practices are followed, in European dating the day precedes the month and year, and Schoenberg frequently used a Roman numeral for the month. In American dating practice, which Schoenberg adopted following his emigration, the month is followed by the day and year. Where no date was provided by the composer, tentative dates based on analysis of the contents have been supplied in square brackets. Suggestion of a provenance where none was indicated originally reflects Schoenberg's residence at the time of origin, unless contraindicated by some detail of the content.

Following the catalog proper are appendixes, a reference list and a general index. **Appendixes**

I. *List of Categories.* A "diplomatic" transcription of Schoenberg's list, described above in the introductory essay, in which the lettering, spacing, and graphic layout of the original is rendered as faithfully as possible in light of common practices of typesetting.

II. *Manuscript List A*. A "diplomatic" transcription which, as far as possible, renders Schoenberg's arrangement of his list. The two portions of the list — that is, the handwritten segment from 1932 and the typewritten one from ca. 1940 (cf. the introductory essay) — are included. The many typing errors in the original of the second portion have been corrected without comment where they involve obvious mechanical errors.

III. *Manuscript List B*. A "diplomatic" transcription of the "List of manuscripts of articles, essays, sketches, etc.," which was made later than Manuscript List A, and which contains reference to items not found on the earlier list. Obvious errors of spelling or typing in the original have been corrected; the order of the original has been preserved. The list was published in Rufer, *Works,* "C. Articles, Essays, Nos. 1 - 141," with numerous changes.

IV. *Alphabetical index of aphorisms entered in the catalog according to short incipit.* The index will facilitate cross references for many aphorisms under different headings, in variant formulations, or in different combinations with other aphorisms.

Reference List Standard biographies of Schoenberg are quoted in the English editions. Shortened references used in the text are in the column to the left of the entry.

General Index Reference is made to persons, institutions, Schoenberg's musical and literary works, theoretical subject matter, artistic techniques, and key areas of Schoenberg's intellectual concerns: teaching, politics, philosophy, criticism. Only those subjects given more than passing mention are included.

Abbreviations Titles in the commentaries have been given shortened form. See the List of References for sigla.

Items that Schoenberg designated for his categories are identified in the catalog by abbreviations using capital letters (viz., "BIO" for "BIOGRAPHISCHES").

A.	Autograph
An.	Anecdotes
ANEK	ANEKDOTEN
APH, or Aph.	APHORISMEN
Art.	Article
AS	Arnold Schoenberg
BIO, or Bio.	BIOGRAPHISCHES
D	Document
Dich.	DICHTUNGEN, TEXTE, SPRÜCHE, APHORISMEN
E.	English
F.	French
Frag.	FRAGMENTE
G.	German
Glossen	GLOSSEN ZU DEN THEORIEN ANDERER
J.Q.	JENS. QUER.
Kl. Ms.	KLEINE MANUSKRIPTE
L.	Letter
Ms.	Manuscript
Ms. List A	Schoenberg's "List of Manuscripts" from 1932 (see Appendix II for transcription)
Ms. List B	Schoenberg's "List of manuscripts of articles, essays, sketches, etc." from the early 1940s (see Appendix III for transcription)
MUS	MUSIKALISCHES
N.	Note
Nb.	Notebook, or NOTEBOOKS
n.d.	no date
n.p.	no provenance
Orch.	ORCHESTRATION
P.	Printed
p.	page(s) with writing
s.	signed
SPR, or Spr.	SPRACHLICHES
T.	Typed
4to	quarto, or A4, approximately 8½ x 11″ and no shorter than 6″
8vo	octavo, approximately 4″ x 5″
16mo	sixteenmo, no longer than approximately 2″ x 3″

PART II A CATALOG

A Catalog of Neglected Items

Biographisches

Designation		Subject	Description
I	1	Printed questionnaire from *Der grosse Herder, Konversationslexikon,* 4th ed. Schoenberg completed the form in black ink but later wrote a note across the face of the document in red pencil concerning the fact that it was never sent. Biographical information and short statements about his artistic intentions as a composer and main principles as a theorist are included as responses to the questions. An excerpt from this item was published in *Gedenkausstellung 1974,* p. 268, without attribution.	P.D.s., with A.N., 1 p., fol., ink, G., *Brookline, Mass., 6.XII.1933;* A.N., pencil, n.p., n.d.
I	2	Proof sheet from the biographical notice written for the 1949 *International Who's Who,* 13th ed.	P.Art, 4 p., 8vo, E., n.p., *July 1948*
II		This collection comprises a conceptual outline of Schoenberg's planned autobiography [ca. 1932] and the later expanded version, two pages of which are dated "January 2, 1944." For the later phase, he prepared many pages of 8vo, 3-holed unlined notebook paper by drawing a vertical line in blue pencil down the left margin of the pages; he attached the original 16mo concept paper to the first of these pages. German and English are mixed. While the idea of the planned work is clear, it is only a sketch. 27 sheets have notations in ink; 9 sheets are empty.	
II	1	"Wie ich Musiker wurde . . ." Small notebook page with lines, attached with tape to the	A.Ms., 1 p., 16mo, ink, G.,

Biographisches

Designation		Subject	Description

first page of item 2a, below. It comprises an outline sketch for an autobiography which includes a list of 4 important transitions in Schoenberg's life; another list of musicians, artists and professionals with whom he associated; and, a short prospectus of the work. This item, called "eine Autobiographie in 'Begegnungen'," can tentatively be dated late 1932. (*See* BIOGRAPHISCHES III, 7.)

n.p., n.d. [Berlin, ca. 1932]

II 2a "Wie ich Musiker wurde . . . "
Four pages which contain a slightly revised list of the important transitions in Schoenberg's life identified in 1, above, followed by lists of about 270 persons and institutions grouped under the following headings: "Meine Freundschaften," "Verleger," "Meine Angehörigen," "Musiker, Maler, Dichter, Schriftsteller," "Music critics and theorists," "Conductors," "Rabbi," "Scientists," "Thiefs," "Schurken," "Mäcene," "Schüler," "Orchestras," "Performers."

4 p., 8vo, G.& E., n.d. [Brentwood, 1944]

2b "Adolph Loos, my friend"
One page with only the above note written across the top.

1 p., n.d.

2c "Is the architect an artist? . . ."
One page commentary on Loos and architecture.

1 p., n.d.

2d One sheet with the names of Josef Rufer, Erwin Ratz, Olga Novakovic written across the top.

1 p., n.d.

2e Thirteen sheets each with one of the following names written at the top: Joseph Polnauer, Heinrich Jalowetz, Erwin Stein, Alban Berg, Albert Einstein, Wasily Kandinsky, Richard Strauss, Gustav Mahler, Alma Mahler Werfel, Franz Werfel, Thomas Mann, Oscar Kokoschka, Karl Kraus.

13 p., n.d.

2f "K. . . . Musikkritiker . . ."
This item comprises a 4to sheet to which an 8vo sheet has been glued. A self-made tab with "KRITIKER" is attached to the upper left corner. The text concerns the music critic "K," of the *Neues Wiener Tagblatt* at the time of Mahler's appointment as Director of the Imperial Opera. Schoenberg ridicules the critic's poor musicianship and writing style.

1 p., n.d.

Biographisches

Designation	Subject	Description

2g "Alexander von Zemlinsky . . ."
The beginning of an essay about Alexander von Zemlinsky, whom Schoenberg met in "about 1894 (or 5?)."

1 p., n.d.

2h "Franz Schreker . . ."
The sheet has a self-made tab on the upper left margin with "COLLEGUES" [*sic*] inscribed on it. The text concerns Franz Schreker, whom Schoenberg esteemed; he names several of Schreker's works he admires.

1 p., *January 2, 1944*

2i "Schurken"
Under this heading Schoenberg makes some comments about Dr. Walter Rubsamen.

1 p., n.d.

2j "UCLA"
Comments about [Robert G.] Sproul.

1 p., *January 2, 1944*

2k "Schurken"
With this heading Schoenberg writes a commentary about a Mr. Milenkovic, a high-ranking official in the Ministry of Culture in pre-World War I Vienna.

2 p., n.d.

III I
BIO
26

"Meine lateinische und meine Kurantschönschrift . . ."
Left and right thumbprints together with handwriting and signature probes with a variety of implements. Facsimile in *Schriften,* p. 396.

A.N.s., 1 p., 8vo, ink & pencil,
G. *Mödling, 28/V. 1923*

III 2
BIO
50

"Ruhe"
Schoenberg regrets his many vehement statements in earlier writings. His excuse was that he reacted to attacks by others (particularly in 1923) and to anti-Semitism. Now (1932) he is more forgiving, for example, toward W[ebern], "meinen einzigen wahren Freund." Letter-head with Nürnberger-Platz address.

A.Ms.s., 1 p., 4to,
ink & pencil, G., *Berlin 20/VII. 1932*

III 3
BIO
60

"Meine Nichtberufung"
As comments on the announcement of efforts to attract foreign students to the Akademie für Musik (recently renamed: Hochschule) in Vienna. He maintains that German music is not esteemed abroad because of "Meister

T.Ms.s., with A.N., 1 p., 8vo, ink, G., *Traunkirchen, 24.VIII.1923;*

*B*iographisches

Designation		Subject	Description
		Strauss." AS's desire to teach almost made him accept a position at the Akademie in spite of reservations. Handwritten glosses, date, and signature. Title in blue crayon pencil apparently added in Berlin, 1932 (see authors' introduction).	A.N., pencil, [Berlin, 1932]
III	4 *BIO* 74	"Sühne" Since the Hofoper, Volksoper, Gesellschaft der Musikfreunde, Konzertverein, and the Philharmoniker in Vienna never performed his works, Schoenberg sets conditions for future requests for permission to perform his music: 1) the directors must be fired; 2) the faults of responsible board members must be published in 3 newspapers. He includes a form with space for the signatures of the new board members. A note ("21.VII.32") states that U[niversal] E[dition] did not comply. Title in blue crayon pencil, apparently added in Berlin, 1932 (see authors' introduction).	A.Ms., 1 p., obl. 8vo, ink G., *Mödling, 15/XI.1923;* A.N.s., ink, G., n.p. [Berlin], *21.VII.32;* A.N., pencil, [Berlin, 1932]
III	5 *BIO* 79	"Mathilde! ich habe mir gelobt . . ." Dedication of the newly-completed text of his *Requiem* to his recently-deceased wife Mathilde. The dedication does not appear in the published version of *Requiem* in *Texte* (1926).	A.N.s., 1 p., 8vo, ink, G., n.p. [Mödling], *15/November 1923*
III	6 *BIO* 82b	"Herr Hofrat Triebenbacher . . ." Response addressed to the above person who was quoted as having said that all evil comes from Jews and the cinema.	T.Ms.s., 2 p., 16mo, G., *Mödling, 15.I.1924;* A.N.s., ink, G., n.p., n.d.
III	7 *BIO* 84	"Lebensgeschichte in Begegnungen / Ich plane seit langem . . ." Schoenberg's idea for his autobiography: not a chronological narrative, but a record of himself as reflected through the interesting persons he had known. For this he planned to collect notes in folders. Eight years later, he dated and signed a heading: "Lebensgeschichte in Begegnungen." (See BIOGRAPHISCHES II, 1.)	T.Ms., 1 p., 8vo, G., *Mödling, 15.Jänner 1924;* A.N.s., ink, G., n.p. [Berlin] *15.VII.32*

Lebensgeschichte in Begegnungen

Ich plane seit langem ,eine Geschichte meines Lebens zu schreiben,wel-
che dadurch zustande kommen soll,dass ich soweit mein Gedächtnis es zu
lässt,alle Menschen,mit denen ich in Berührung gekommen bin,soweit sie
und ihr Verhältnis zu mir interessant sind ,so darstelle,wie sich mir
gezeigt haben und genau erzähle in welchen Bezfehungen wir zu einander gestanden sind.Natürlich ist das nicht in erster Linie ein Racheakt
sondern wirklich bloss ein System sein,von welchen ich mir verspreche,
dass es mein Gedächtnis erschliessen wird.Es werden sich von Person z
zu Person die Glieder finden und die Ereignisse und so glaube ich wirk+
lich so wahrhaftig zu werden,als es nur irgend möglich ist;während der
Versuch einer chronologischen Darstellung mir unbedingt misslingen dürf
te.Für viele nun allerdings wird dieses Buch notwendiger weise eine sch
schwere und ich glaube,verdiente Strafe werden.Denn ich werde hier nict
mildern können,sondern nur ein Bestreben haben:so wahr als möglich zu
sein.
An die Ausführung werde ich sehr bald herangehen und denke dabei fol-
gendermassen zu verfahren.
Ich werde in Form einer Kartothek Umschläge oder kleine Mappen bereits
stellen und allmählich Notizen sammeln,die ich mir so wie sie mir ein-
fallen;aufschreiben werde;zwanglos,ohne Programm.Diese Notizen wedre ic
ich oft durchsehen,Vormerkungen über Personen und Ereignisse an geeig-
neter Stelle machen und schliesslich allmählich soweit kommen,dass ich
einzelnen Partien eine geschlossene Form gebe.Im ganzen allerdings gla
be ich,dass die aphoristische die geeignetste sein wird.Mindestens so
lange,als nicht wenigstens irgend ein Zeitabschnitt oder eine Personen
gruppe als abgeschlossen angesehen werden kann.
Mödling,15.Jänner 1924

[handwritten signature and date 15.VII.72]

BIO III, 7. Schoenberg's commentary on his planned autobiography. The handwritten title and commentary was added during the composer's organization of his papers in Berlin, 1932.

Biographisches

Designation		Subject	Description
III	8	"Nochmals Sühne"	T.Ms.s., 2 p.,
	BIO	Looking forward to his 50th birthday (13 September	fol., G.,
	89a-b	1924), AS makes some conditions pertaining to possible	*Mödling,*
		celebratory performances: since the 5 large musical	*17. Februar*
		organizations in Vienna have neglected his works	*1924;* A.N.,
		completely, no permissions will be given until responsible	ink & pencil,
		persons have been identified. The good, but badly-	[Berlin, 1932]

III · 8 · continued:

Looking forward to his 50th birthday (13 September 1924), AS makes some conditions pertaining to possible celebratory performances: since the 5 large musical organizations in Vienna have neglected his works completely, no permissions will be given until responsible persons have been identified. The good, but badly-directed, Philharmonic programed *Verklärte Nacht,* but did not play it because of the stipulation that it could only be played by orchestras which had performed the orchestral works first. Schoenberg's friend "P" (Pieau?, see BIOGRAPHISCHES III, 35) informs him that the Gesellschaft der Musikfreunde did program *Gurre-Lieder,* but did not perform it because of insufficient rehearsal time.

Title in ink apparently added in Berlin, 1932 (see authors' introduction).

(The title refers to BIOGRAPHISCHES III, 4, above.)

III	9	"50ter"	*T.Ms.s., 1 p.,*
	BIO	"Man hat mir offen anvertraut . . ."	*fol., G.,*
	92	Preface to *Arnold Schönberg zum fünfzigsten*	*Mödling,*
		Geburtstage, 13. September 1924 (Sonderheft der	*20. August*
		Musikblätter des Anbruch, 6. Jahrg., Aug.-Sept., 1924,	*1924;* A.N.,
		Vienna).	pencil & ink,
		Title in blue crayon pencil apparently added in Berlin,	[Berlin, 1932]
		1932 (see authors' introduction).	

III	10	"Inschrift für *Trude* in der Harmonielehre"	A.Ms., 1 p.,
	BIO	Inscription to Trude [Schoenberg's wife, Gertrud	16mo, glued
	95	Schoenberg] for her copy of the 1921 edition of the	to face of 8vo,
		Harmonielehre. It is the same as the inscription written	ink, G., n.p.,
		into the bound copy described by Rufer, *Works,* p. 133,	n.d. [1924]
		with the date *25.VIII.1924.* Ms. List A: no. 95, dated	
		"1924."	

III	11	"Polytonales bei mir"	T.Ms., 2 p.,
	BIO	Essay on the incidence of polytonality in Schoenberg's	obl. 16mo,
	100B	own works. He names the early Lieder, op. 1, no. 2 and	G., n.p.
		op. 3, no. 3, the *Kammersymphonie,* and *Pelleas und*	[Mödling],
		Melisande, op. 7. This is a copy of an item under AS's	*12 / XII.*
		category "Musikalisches." His designation on the first	*1924;*
		page, "Mus / 100B," is apparently an error; see Ms. List	A.N., pencil
		A: no. 100A reads "Mus"; no. 100B reads "Bio."	[Berlin, 1932]

Biographisches

Designation	Subject	Description

Title in pencil is apparently added in Berlin, 1932 (see authors' introduction).

III 12 *BIO* *108*	"Ich habe einerseits . . ." Schoenberg comments on his poor memory for faces and its effect on his ability to draw portraits.	A.Ms.s., 1 p., 16mo, ink, G., n.p. [Berlin], *1/6. 1926*
III 13 *BIO* *111ᵇ*	"Aufklärung über mein Verhältnis zu *R. Strauss*" A short essay which concerns some possible mutual misunderstanding between Schoenberg and Strauss. AS indicates his intention of deleting his remark about modern composers who pose as Don Juans from his earlier article (published as "Probleme des Kunst-unterrichtes," in *Schriften,* pp. 165-78, and *SI* 75, pp. 365-69). In a note Schoenberg writes: "Abschrift von *111ᵇ bei Aph*"; but the 111ᵇ is apparently an error. It should be 111ᵃ, as indicated on his Ms. List A: no. 111a reads "Aph, Rich Strauss, 23/V. 1926"; no. 111b is marked "Bio" and "Abschrift" and dated "21.VII.32." (See APHORISMEN I, 15, "Aph. 111ᵃ.")	A.Ms.s., 1 p., 8vo, ink, G., n.p. [Berlin], *23.V.1926;* A.N., n.p., n.d. [Berlin, July 21, 1932]
III 14 *BIO* *115*	"Feuilleton / Erinnerungen an *Bösendorfer.* Von Ludwig *Karpath.*" Clipping from unidentified newspaper with story by Ludwig Karpath. The article (dated "18. Oktober") is underlined in pencil. Attached to the margins are small pieces of paper with glosses in which AS comments on the man Bösendorfer and his concert hall, the site of a very mixed reception of *Verklärte Nacht* (18 March 1902). AS recalls that Karpath and other critics threatened Webern who applauded the 2nd string Quartet at the first performance in 1907. Remarks about Bösendorfer inspire gloss on verso: *"Karpath als Faschist!"*	P.Art. with A.N., 2 p., obl. 4to ink, G., *Roquebrune,* *Oktober, 1928*
III 15 *BIO* *124*	"ARNOLD / Endlich allein!" Commentary on Schoenberg's own (welcome) artistic isolation. Features a doodle on "Arnold."	A.Ms.s., 1 p., 8vo, ink, G., n.p. [Berlin] *4.II.1928*
III 16 *BIO* *134*	"Glocken am Thury" AS writes that when church bells interfered with his composing in Vienna, 1903-09, Mahler was unsympa-	A.Ms.s., 2 p., obl. 8vo, ink G., n.p.

Biographisches

Designation		Subject	Description
		thetic to his complaint. Later, when Mahler complained that birds were disturbing him, Schoenberg remarked that destiny always avenges offensive behavior.	[Berlin], *21.VII.1932*
III	17 *BIO* *135*	"Das Tempo der Entwicklung" AS, commenting on a remark by an unidentified French critic about his development, distinguishes between himself and the makers of new fashions: Milhaud, Poulenc, Stravinsky.	A.Ms., 1 p., 8vo, ink, G., *Roquebrune, wahrscheinlich 1928*
III	18 *BIO* *149*	"Beantwortung wissenschaftlicher Fragen" Answer to questionnaire posed by the psychologist Julius Bahle. Published in English translation in Reich, *Schoenberg,* pp. 236-42, with the date "early in 1931."	T.Ms., with A.N. in ink, 8 p., 4to, carbon, G., *Berlin, vielleicht 1928* [or 1931]
III	19 *BIO* *161*	"Schaffensqual" Schoenberg, responding to an accusation of creative inhibition, describes his creative process: in general, he writes very little, but very fast. List of works composed in a short time includes *Erwartung,* the 2nd and 3rd String Quartets, *Gurre-Lieder, Pierrot, Jakobsleiter* (Part I). A note on the front, "Abschrift, Original v[on] 7.4.28. Mus 161," was apparently added in 1932 (see authors' introduction).	T.Ms., 2 p., 8vo, G., n.p. [Berlin], *7.4.28;* A.N., pencil, G., [Berlin, 1932]
III	20 *BIO* *237b*	"Bei der Erstaufführung meiner *Variationen* . . ." On the day of the first performance of the *Variations,* 2 December 1928, Schoenberg had a sudden indisposition, which, he explained, originated in the scandalous reception of the performance taking place at the same hour in Berlin, some distance away. Schoenberg notes that he has placed a copy of the Ms. with the papers in "Denkmäler": "Abschrift von 237 bei Denk (Rückseite)." In addition we find: "Siehe auch An[ekdoten]."	A.Ms.s., 1 p., obl. 8vo, ink, G., *Berlin, 16.X.1929;* A.N., ink, G., n.p. [Berlin], *22.VII.32*
III	21 *BIO* *281*	"An die Int.[ernationale] Ges.[ellschaft] f.[ür] neue Musik . . ." Draft for a letter to the International Society for New	A.L., 2 p., obl. 16mo, pencil, G.,

Biographisches

Designation		Subject	Description
		Music requesting that his Woodwind Quintet be withdrawn from the festival. AS complains about the insulting treatment by President Edward Dent in 1925. Ms. List A: no. 281, dated "etwa 1926."	n.p. [Berlin], n.d. [ca. 1926]
III	22 *BIO* 285	"P.T. Univ. Edition / Lieber Herr Direktor . . ." Letter concerning a number and variety of issues: royalties for performances, 2nd ed. of the *Harmonielehre,* Schoenberg's relationship with [Wilhelm] Hansen (he prefers U.E. – if they would be reasonable), [Paul] Pella's request to perform *Gurre-Lieder* in Berlin. He wants to please Pella and [Heinrich] Jalowetz and not offend [Paul] Scheinpflug. At the top AS notes that the letter was never sent. At the bottom he comments that the letter is confused because at the time of writing it he was an inexperienced writer who forgot his sentences while writing them down.	T.L.s., 4 p., fol., G., *Mödling, 22.II.1923;* A.N., ink, n.p. [Berlin], *3.VIII.32*
III	23 *BIO* 289	"Die letzte Vision Adolphe Willettes" [clipping] Small sheet with attached clipping from the evening edition of the *Berliner Tageblatt* (dated by Schoenberg "5.II.1926."). The notations indicate that the incident in the news report reminded AS of a scene (the death and transformation of "Der Sterbende") from his own oratorio *Die Jakobsleiter.* Excerpt in translation in Ringer, "Faith and Symbol," *JASI* 6/1 (June 1982): 83-84.	P.Art. with A.N.s., 1 p., obl. 16mo, ink, G., n.p., *5.II.1926*
III	24 *BIO* 295	"Interview mit Arnold Schönberg von Jens Qu. Man mag über Schönberg denken . . ." AS interviewed by his alter ego, Jens Qu[er]. Topic is music-making in Berlin. Draft for BIOGRAPHISCHES III, 26 ("BIO / 306") below, dated "*13.III.1925.*"	A.Ms., 1 p., obl. 8vl, ink, G., n.p. [Mödling], n.d. [early 1925]
III	25 *BIO* 296	"Ich habe in dieser Zeit . . ." Typed note glued together with news clipping from unidentified newspaper and an autograph note. Schoenberg was inspired to comment on a paragraph in the clipping which begins "Arnold Schönberg, der Führer der Expressionisten in der Musik." The comment was addressed to the editor of *Anbruch.*	P.Art. with T.N.s, 1 p., obl. 16mo, G.; A.N., ink, n.p., n.d.

Biographisches

Designation		Subject	Description
III	26	"Sehr geehrter Herr . . ."	T.Ms., 1 p.,
	BIO	The beginning of a humorous article featuring the	fol., G., *Wien*
	306	composer and his alter ego, Jens Quer. Note in green	*3.III.1923,*
		pencil: "Anfang eines humoristischen Artikels für	with A.N.s.,
		'Pult und Taktstock' / Jens Qu. interpoliert Arnold	pencil,
		Schönberg." Notes in red pencil: "Siehe 295 bei *Bio,*" and	*Mödling,*
		"1925?" (See BIOGRAPHISCHES III, 24, above.)	*5.III.1925,*
			13.III.1925,
			1925?
III	27	"Lieber Alex, erinnerst du dich . . ."	A.L.s. with
	BIO	Letter to Alexander v. Zemlinsky in answer to a question	musical
	319	about the technique of composing with 12 tones. In his	notation, 1 p.,
		reply, AS includes the opening measures of the *Suite,* op.	fol., pencil,
		29, indicating that the four 6-part chords can be	G., *Mödling,*
		interpreted as "I - IV - V - I. — Ouverture" ("Du siehst[,]	*17.VI.1925;*
		das geht also auch"). He mentions that the 2nd and 3rd	A.N.s., ink,
		movements are already finished and that they are based	G., n.p.
		on the same row as the opening. Zemlinsky's reply to the	[Berlin],
		letter is found in the Library of Congress.	*8/8. 32*
		In August 1932, Schoenberg noted on the present draft	
		that he had come to realize that Zemlinsky's question was	
		meant to irritate him.	
III	28	"Aus 'Giacomo Puccini Intimi'"	P.Art. with
	BIO	The item is the clipping of an article by Guido Marotti	A.N., 4 p.,
	334	and Ferrucio Pagni which quotes Puccini's remarks about	8vo, ink, G.,
		Schoenberg on the occasion of the tour with *Pierrot* in	n.p., n.d.
		Italy, 1924. AS's Ms. List A: no. 334, dated "1930?"	[after 1926]
III	29	"Malerische Einflüsse"	A.Ms.s., 3 p.,
	BIO	AS's reply to his biographer Paul Stefan regarding an	ink, G.,
	350	alleged influence from Kokoschka. Published in facsimile	*Los Angeles,*
		in *JASI* 2/3 (June 1978): 233-35, with an English	*11.II.1938*
		translation, pp. 237-38.	
III	30	*"Meine Gegner"*	A.Ms., 2 p.,
	BIO	Schoenberg finds contradictions in the arguments of his	8vo, ink, G.,
	355	opponents: according to them his music is both German	n.p. [Berlin],
		and international, "Kultur-Bolschewik" and bourgeois;	*5.X. 1932,*
		he is considered a Jew, but his students and closest	*6.X. 1933*

Biographisches

Designation	Subject	Description

colleagues are Aryans. Date at end, "6.X.1933," is apparently an error. See Ms. List A: Bio 355, dated "X, 5 32."

This essay is not the same as the portion of "Neue Musik/Meine Musik" entitled "IV/*Meine Gegner,*" published in *JASI* 1/2 (February 1977): 108-10.

30
Cover

Cover for item 30, above. "Bio 355" written on front.

1 p., 8vo, pencil

III **31** *BIO 356*

"Diebe"
Schoenberg discusses those who have "robbed" him. The list of names is divided into "a) an meinem Ueberfluss" and "b) an meinem Mangel." In the first he places Hauer, for example, and in the second, Hertzka. He concentrates on Hertzka's unfair treatment in connection with the Bach Choralvorspiele and *Gurre-Lieder.* (See BIOGRAPHISCHES III, 32.)

A.Ms., 1 p., 8vo, ink, G., n.p, n.d.

III **32** *BIO 361*

"----an meinem Ueberfluss"
In AS's category "Denkmäler" he will expose those who had robbed him of a) his "Ueberfluss" and b) his "Mangel." An example of those in group a) is the "Hochmeister des Deutschen Ordens," who seized AS's solution to the economic crisis (i.e., making industrial workers become farmers). Includes a note on the "*recht*zeitigen" Nazi, Walter Grossbach.

A.Ms.s., 2 p., 8vo, ink, G., n.p. [Berlin], *12.XI.1932*

32
Cover

Cover for item 32, above. "BIO 361" written on front.

1 p., 8vo, pencil

III **33** *BIO 372*

"Sind das nur Rangesfragen?"
Extended commentary on the inhibition of intellectual communication caused by social discrimination at a formal reception arranged by the Academy of Arts in Berlin, hosted by the (arrogant) Prof. Amersdorfer. Includes an evaluation of Max v. Schillings' shallow attitude. AS ridicules the insensitive remarks about his music at such receptions and states his belief in the cultural mission of the lower classes. In a later note written in 1933 after Schillings' anti-Semitic attack on him, AS confesses that he earlier had believed that Hitler could be stopped.
On the back cover is an aphorism ("31.XII.32"): "Klugheit kann niemals das Ausserordentliche hervorbringen."

A.Ms.s., 5 p., 8vo, ink, G., n.p. [Berlin], *19.XI.1932;* Brookline, [Mass.], *27.XII.1933;* A.Ms., ink, G., *31.XII.32*

Biographisches

Designation		Subject	Description
III	34 *BIO* *379*	"Lieber Freund, dieser Brief . . ." Draft for letter to Mengelberg, self-bound. Concerns AS's conditions for accepting the presidency of the Mahler Society. Published in transcription and English translation in Türcke, "Mahler Society," *JASI* 7/1 (June 1983): 78-85.	A.L.s., 6p., fol. pencil, G., n.p., *1920 oder 21/* *vor Mussolini* *11. September* [1920]
	34 Cover	Cover with title: "MAHLER BUND / BRIEF AN MENGELBERG / enthaltend 'Demokratie'" The title in black crayon pencil is apparently written in Brentwood, ca. 1940 (see authors' introduction).	A.D., fol., pencil, n.p., *1921 od[er] 22,* [Brentwood, ca. 1940]
III	35 *BIO* *380*	"Mein armer Freund Walter P. . . ." Biographical data about Schoenberg's friend Walter P[ieau], with memories of joyful, Bohemian days 30 years back. Note at bottom indicates that Pieau, whom AS thought dead, had visited him "vor ungefähr einem halben Jahr." Ms. List A: no. 380, "Walter Pieau-Freund meiner Jugend," dated, "vielleicht 26?"	A.Ms., 1 p., 4to, pencil G., n.p., n.d. [1926?]; A.N.s., n.p., n.d.
III	36 *BIO* *381*	"Das Vorwort ist von mir" Schoenberg's preface, published in E. Stein, *Praktischer Leitfaden zu Schönbergs Harmonielehre* (Universal Edition, 1912/22). The note at the top apparently dates from Brentwood, ca. 1940 (see authors' introduction). Another note in black crayon is found at the bottom of the page: "Vorwort zum Führer durch die Harmonielehre von Erwin Stein."	T.Ms.s., 1 p., 4to, carbon, G., n.p., n.d.; A.N., pencil, [Brentwood, ca. 1940]
III	37 *BIO* *387*	"REPUTATION?" Schoenberg has clipped an announcement from an unidentified newspaper about his teaching position at USC; the item is dated 25 August 1935. He adds a critical comment inspired by a statement about his status as a modern composer. The title in black crayon pencil apparently dates from Brentwood, ca. 1940 (see authors' introduction).	P.Art., with A.Ms., 16mo, 2 p., pencil, E., n.p. [Hollywood], *August 25,* *1935;* A.N., pencil [Brentwood, ca. 1940]

Biographisches

Designation			Subject	Description
III	38 *BIO* *391*		Original and carbon copy of public announcement by AS. The designation "BIO 391," as well as a heading, "ANKÜNDIGUNG," is written on the copy.	
	38.1		"Arnold Schönberg[,] der im Begriff ist . . ." Brief presentation of Schoenberg as author of theoretical works, followed by an announcement of classes in analysis (at USC?). Three classes are offered: I. Classical music to ca. 1900; II. New music (1900-1934); III. Bad music ("Schlechte Musik") from all periods. The fee is one dollar per lecture and a schedule is indicated. Ms. List A: no. 391, date "1934 or 35."	T.D., 1 p., 4to, G., n.p., n.d. [Hollywood, 1934?]
	38.2		"ANKÜNDIGUNG/ Arnold Schönberg[,] der im Begriff ist . . ." Heading and designation in black crayon pencil apparently added in Brentwood, ca. 1940 (see authors' introduction).	T.D., 1 p., 4to, carbon; A.N., pencil, [Brentwood, ca. 1940]
III	39 *BIO* *393*		*"Mein Gesuch um Zulassung als Privatdozent"* Schoenberg evaluates the letters from Mahler, Karl Goldmark, and F. Löwe which supported his application for a position as a Privat-Dozent at the Music Academy in Vienna (1910). Mahler's letter was quite cool; Löwe's reminds AS of Löwe's rejection of the *Kammersymphonie* in 1906 and of Bruckner's criticism of Löwe. Bound in a self-made cover. Together with newspaper clipping from *Neues Wiener Journal,* dated "15. Juni 1932," in which the mentioned letters are published. A fourth letter, from Weingartner, was not published, as both AS and the author withheld permission. Autograph note in unknown hand: "Das wollte ich dir damals schicken. Kennst du es?"	A.Ms., 3 p., 8vo, ink, pencil, G., n.p. [Berlin], *30. VIII.1932.* Together with clipping, 1 p., fol., G., *15. Juni 1932;* A.N. in unknown hand, n.p., n.d.
III	40 *BIO* *396*		*"Max Liebermann—wenn ich nicht irre, . . ."* Inspired by Liebermann's 85th birthday, AS draws a distinction between the painter's artistic intelligence (which AS admires) and his conventional philosophy.	A.Ms.s., 2 p., 8vo, ink, G., n.p. [Berlin],

Biographisches

Designation		Subject	Description
		Subsequent extensive notes, dated separately, comment on Liebermann's concern about the absence of tradition in AS's music. AS quotes Mahler: "Tradition ist Schlamperei."	*20.VII.1932; 27.VIII.1932; 29.VIII.1932*
	40 Cover	Cover for commentary on Max Liebermann, 40 above. "396 BIO" written on front.	1 p., 8vo, pencil
III	41 *BIO* *400*	*"Die Priorität"* The item comprises an essay with a self-made cover. Subsequent additions to the text are dated separately. Schoenberg is concerned with establishing priorities in the development of 12-tone compositional techniques. It involves polemics against Webern, on matters of racism and falsification of dates of his early works, and against Hauer, whose 12-tone theory did not emerge, as did AS's, from the development of the necessary technical means.	A.Ms.s., 8 p., 8vo, ink & pencil, G., n.p. [Brentwood], *10.IX.1932, 11.9.1932, 11.IX.1932*
III	42 *BIO* *405*	"Ich sende Ihnen hier ein paar Tatsachen . . ." Draft for letter. Marginal gloss at "Ihnen" in opening indicates that it was meant for [J.] Rufer or [E.] Stein. Concerns critics who reacted hysterically or stupidly to AS's works: Richard Heuberger (*Verklärte Nacht*); Hans L.; Robert Hirschfeld; Herr St. (*Pelleas*); Dr. B. (*Kammersymphonie*); Max Kalbeck (2nd String Quartet). Examples of musical invective. Ms. List A: no. 405, dated "1929?" Pencil note reads: "Copy under Doubletten."	T.L. with A.N., 1 p, 4to, pencil, G., n.p., n.d. [ca. 1929]
III	43 *BIO* *407*	"Arnold Schönbergs Berliner Konzertskandal von Alban Berg" Newspaper clipping from *Neues W[iener] Journal,* dated by AS "4.12.28," with glosses on separate piece, both of which are glued to a piece of music Ms. paper. Schoenberg corrects Berg who neglected the fact that Furtwängler conducted works by AS in Berlin ca. 8 years before (though not as early as Nikisch, who conducted the *Kammersymphonie* in 1914). Schoenberg disagrees with Berg: in his opinion an audience has no right to applaud as it can not be held responsible for its mistakes. It should remain silent.	P.Art. with A.N., 1 p., obl. 4to, ink, G., n.p. [Berlin], *4.12.28*

Biographisches

Designation		Subject	Description

III   44
BIO
408

"Krach um Schönberg"
Fragmentary comments in response to the review of Furtwängler's performance of the *Variations for Orchestra,* op. 31, with the Berliner Philharmonic (2 December 1928). Clipping titled "Krach um Schönberg" is signed R.K. One note concerns the concept of "Verstandesmusik" (see DICHTUNGEN 4 a, below). In another note AS ruefully remarks that only his works with texts have been public successes.

P.Art.
attached to
4to sheet with
A.N., 1 p.,
8vo, ink,
G., n.p.
n.d. [Berlin,
ca. 1928]

III   45.1
BIO
416

"Es gibt kein Entrinnen:"
Schoenberg's elaborate practical joke. Having made a little toy (called: "Vexier-Etui"), which presents a perpetual problem of opening, he declares it to be one of his best works in a humorous essay. It is his opinion that future music historians will claim that if this object is his "best," the rest (that is, his musical works) must be of lesser value. The toy is in the legacy; the essay is written on a sheet of stationery and glued to a matching envelope embossed with the Brentwood address.

A.Ms.s., 2 p.,
obl. 16mo,
ink, G.,
Los Angeles,
4. Mai 1940

45.2

"There is no escape . . ."
Translation of the above essay into English.
Listed on Ms. List B: no. 91.

T.Ms.s., 1 p.,
8vo, E.,
July 29, 1940

III   46
BIO
417

"Nicht mehr ein Deutscher"
On the problems facing a German composer abroad and at home. Mentions the "Hegemonie" of German art. Draft for preface to *Drei Satiren,* op. 28, published in 1926.

A.Ms., 1 p.,
16mo, pencil,
G., n.p., n.d.
[1925 or 26],
glued to front
of T.N., 1 p.,
obl. 8vo, G.,
n.p., n.d.

III   47.1
BIO
418

"Da ich aus bekannten Grunden . . ."
Draft for a circular letter explaining that AS's membership of the German Society of Composers was cancelled when he left Germany in May of 1933; hence, he no longer received royalties for performances. Also, his application for membership to the Austrian Society of Authors, Composers, and Music Publishers ("AKM") was rejected because of conflict concerning royalties while

A.Ms., 2 p.,
fol, pencil,
G., n.p., n.d.
[Hollywood,
ca. 1935]

Biographisches

Designation	Subject	Description
	a member, ca. 1920. Receivers of the letter are requested to account for performances of his works since the beginning of 1934 and to send royalties to the composer. Ms. List A: no. 418, dated "about 1935 or 6."	
47.2	English translation of the above.	A.Ms., 3 p., 4to, pencil, E., n.p., n.d. [Hollywood, ca. 1935]
47.3	French translation of 47.1; contains only the first paragraph.	A.Ms., 1 p., 4to, pencil, F., n.p., n.d. [Hollywood, ca. 1935]
47 Cover	Self-made hard-paper cover with dividers for items 47, 1-3, above. Title: (Geplantes) RUNDSCHREIBEN BESCHWERDE WEGEN A K M a) deutsch b) englisch (Fragment) c) französisch " The designation "BIO 418" is written on front.	A.D., fol., pencil, [Hollywood, ca. 1935]
III 48 BIO 419A	"Although engaged as University professor, . . ." Handwritten draft for telegram to Artur Schnabel. Schoenberg, in desperate need of a visa, requests help in finding an engagement in England or elsewhere. Published in Stuckenschmidt, *Schoenberg,* p. 410. Doodle: the 5 lines of a staff delineate 4 "fingers" of a hand.	A.N., 1 p., 4to, pencil, E., n.p., n.d. [Hollywood, ca. 1935]
III 49 BIO 419B	"Dear Mr. Van Klein-Smid:" Draft for letter concerning payment for lectures at USC, fall of 1935. AS feels exploited, as he expected a larger	A.L., 2 p., 4to, pencil, E.,

Biographisches

Designation		Subject	Description
		share of student fees than the $138 he received. He also complains about the lack of publicity at USC.	n.p., n.d. [Hollywood, ca. 1935]
	48-49 Cover	Cover for above 2 items with a list of contents: 　　A) WITHOUT A PERMANENT VISA / 　　　　DECEMBER 1935 　　B) LETTER TO A GOOD BUSINESSMAN "BIO 419" is found on the cover.	A.S., 1 p., 4to, pencil E., n.p. [Hollywood], *1933-DECEMBER 1935*
III	50.1 *BIO 425*	*"Satz wie Liedertexte / Vorwort"* "Die Gurre-Lieder habe ich anfangs 1900 komponiert . . ." Three sheets bound together on left side with drafts for AS's program notes for a performance on 14 January 1910, which included the *George Lieder,* op. 15, Part I of the *Gurre-Lieder,* songs from opp. 2 and 6, and the *Piano Pieces,* op. 11. The second page is an extensive draft for the part of the notes that concerns the lack of understanding of new artistic ideals. AS quotes Schopenhauer and reviews the apathy and wickedness of his opponents. The last page contains deleted sketches for the beginning of the notes. A note in blue pencil reads: "Webern / [Rudolf] Weirich aufs Program." The notes are published in Maegaard, *Studien,* vol. 2, p. 123f.; translation in Reich, *Schoenberg,* p. 48. Ms. List A: no. 425, dated "1908."	A.Ms.s., 3 p., fol., pencil, G., n.p., n.d., [Vienna, 1910]
III	50.2	A carbon copy of the first sheet, above (50.1). Notes in black crayon pencil: "Doubletten" (at the top); "copy / under BIO 425" (at the bottom).	A.Ms.s., 1 p., fol. carbon, [Vienna, 1910]
IV	1.1	"Als Schönberg einige Monate in Barcelona lebte . . ." In a short essay Schoenberg expresses his opinion about how little his place of residence affects his composition. Refers to his period in Barcelona in 1931 when he composed the second act of *Moses und Aron:* In any climate two times two is four ("Zweimal zwei ist in jedem Klima vier").	T.Ms., 1 p., 8vo, G., n.p., n.d. [after 1933]

*B*iographisches

Designation		Subject	Description

<table>
<tr><td></td><td>1.2</td><td>When for eight months I lived in Barcelona . . ."
Translation of the above statement. Typed note across the top: "Printed in the Los Angeles Times, pg. 5, part IV / Sunday, May 14, 1950." "Arnold Schoenberg" is typed at the bottom.
On the back is a revised version of the first half of the German original (item 1.1); apparently by Gertrud Schoenberg: "Als wir 8 Monate in Barcelona verlebten. . . ."</td><td>T.Ms.s. [typed], 1 p., 4to, carbon, E., Los Angeles [Brentwood] April 19, 1950; with A.N. on the back in unknown hand, ink, G., n.d.</td></tr>
<tr><td></td><td>1.3</td><td>Clipping from the Los Angeles Times Music Section, Sunday, 14 May 1950, part 4, p. 5, "The Sounding Board," a column by Alert Goldberg: "The Transplanted Composer," features photographs of Stravinsky, Castelnuovo-Tedesco, and Schoenberg. Includes the translation, 1.2, above.</td><td>P.Art., 1 p., fol, E., Los Angeles [Brentwood], May 14, 1950</td></tr>
<tr><td>V</td><td>1</td><td>"K.ung. Honved Ministerium — Budapest"
Draft for letter to Austro-Hungarian military authorities. Written before Schoenberg's review, which was scheduled in April-May 1915, the letter requests special consideration ("Einjährigen-Recht") on the basis of artistic and educational merits: he explains that he is ranked among the 10 greatest living composers (lists capitals where his works have been heard), his Harmonielehre is a major theoretical work, he is listed in recent reference works (e.g., Riemann's Musikgeschichte), and has taught at the Royal Academy of Music, Vienna (as Privat-Dozent).</td><td>A.L., 2 p., fol., ink, G., n.p., n.d. [Berlin, early 1915]</td></tr>
<tr><td>V</td><td>2</td><td>"SCHÖNBERG, Professor Arnold . . ."
Professional résumé. Records biographical data, main compositions (up to Variations for Orchestra, op. 31), and publications.</td><td>T.D., 1 p., 8vo, carbon, G., Berlin-Charlottenburg, n.d. [ca. 1928]</td></tr>
</table>

Biographisches

Designation		Subject	Description
V	3	"This is the revised order . . ." Addenda for biographical résumé, which revises list of publications extending from *Harmonielehre,* 1911, to "Counterpoint, vol. I (unfinished)." This last entry was later changed to "Counterpoint in 3 volumes . . ." of which vol. 3 is incomplete. (*Preliminary Exercises in Counterpoint* was finished in 1942 and published after Schoenberg's death.) Pencil notes by Schoenberg's assistant Leonard Stein add a few titles.	T.D. with A.N., 1 p., 4to, E., ink & pencil, n.p., n.d. [Brentwood, ca. 1950]
V	4.1-2	"Arnold Schoenberg, composer, teacher . . ." Autobiographical summary from date of birth to 1940. Includes family relations, books published until 1942, selected compositions until 1943. Typed "addenda," on one of the two copies only, list theoretical works, including *Style and Idea* (1950).	T.D., 2 p., 4to, carbon, E., *Los Angeles* [Brentwood], n.d. [ca. 1944]; T.N., E., n.p., n.d. [Brentwood, ca. 1950]
V	5	"Zeittafel zu Arnold Schoenbergs Biographie" Important events in Schoenberg's life are listed: compositions until 1949, theory books, teaching experience. On p. 2 are entries added in ink (by Gertrud Schoenberg?) and pencil (by Leonard Stein).	T.D., 2 p., 4to, carbon G., n.p. [Brentwood], *November 26, 1949*
V	6	"ARNOLD SCHOENBERG, composer . . ." Professional résumé which includes education (begins with public school in Vienna), positions (until 1940, UCLA), students in Europe and USA, published books, compositions. An addendum lists the publications in theory. Brentwood address stamped twice at top of page. Marginal note: "PLEASE RETURN AT ONCE."	T.D., 3 p., 4to, carbon, E., *Los Angeles* [Brentwood], n.d. [ca. 1949]
V	7	"BIOGRAPHY / vaccination certificate . . ." Biographical summary in third person (possibly by Gertrud Schoenberg). From AS's childhood to his 75th birthday (13 September 1949). Brief notes without explicative details, mostly of a strictly personal nature.	T.D., 2 p., 4to, carbon, E., *Los Angeles,* n.d. [Brentwood, ca. 1950]

Biographisches

Designation	Subject	Description
8.1	"Gentlemen . . ." The original draft for an autobiographical letter describing AS's health from childhood to 1950 in great detail: includes a record of smoking habits, and a description of his "death" ("Todesfall"), or the cardiac arrest suffered in August 1946.	T.L., 2 p., fol., E., n.p. [Brentwood] *August 2, 1950*
8.2-3	"Gentlemen . . ." Carbon copy of the above letter, with a second carbon of page one.	T.L., 3 p., 4to, carbon

Fragmente

Designation	Subject	Description
I 92	Collection of literary fragments, dating from Vienna, ca. 1900, bound together with brads into one volume. The number "92," found on several items, corresponds to Schoenberg's entry on Ms. List B: no. 92, "Seven Fragments A-G, no dates, but probably before 1900."	
I 1 92 Cover	"*SIEBEN FRAGMENTE* / (Erste schriftstellerische Versuche)" Title page with the table of contents from A-G:	T.D., 1 p., 8vo, G., n.p., n.d.

A Einige Ideen zur Begründung einer modernen Kompositions-lehre

B Wer spricht[,] wünscht T(h)eilnahme zu finden

C Das Opern- und Konzertpublikum und seine Führer (Disposition)

D Dasselbe eine halbe Seite des Anfangs

E Entwurf des "Programms" zu einer symphonischen Dichtung "HANS IM GLUECK"

F Durchstrichener Beginn eines Programms zu "Pelleas und Melisande von Maeterlinck"

G Anscheinend ein Versuch[,] eine Musikschule finanziell aufzubauen

FRAG I, 5. A page from possibly the earliest manuscript in Schoenberg's literary legacy.

Fragmente

Designation		*Subject*	*Description*

| I | 2 | "Einige Ideen zur Begründung . . ." | A.Ms., 2 p., |
| *92* | *A* | Schoenberg writes that the starting point for a composition is not a theme or a motif, but the urge to project ideas and beliefs which lie beyond the sphere of matter ("ausserhalb des Stofflichen"). Simple imitation of nature is not adequate to the task which calls for artistic formulation, the first step of which is stylization. | fol., pencil, G., n.p., n.d. [Vienna, ca. 1900] |

| I | 3 | "Wer spricht[,] wünscht Aufmerksamkeit . . ." | A.Ms., 1 p., |
| *92* | *B* | A simple message of immediate interest will capture the listener's attention and does not require artistic interpolation. This is apparently a draft for "A," above. | fol., pencil, G., n.p., n.d. [Vienna, ca. 1900] |

| I | 4 | "Das Opern- und Konzertpublikum . . ." | A.Ms., 1 p., |
| *92* | *C* | Schoenberg writes an outline for an essay on the role of the audience in the art scene. Influential factors: critics, performers-as-critics, dilettantes, printed programs. | fol., pencil, G., n.p., n.d. [Vienna, ca. 1900] |

| I | 5 | *"Das Opern- und Concertpublikum . . ."* | A.Ms., 1 p., |
| *92* | *D* | Short essay on a topic related to "C" above. It concerns the lack of unifying styles at the end of the previous century ("im letzten Viertel dieses Jahrhunderts"). | fol., pencil, G., n.p., n.d. [Vienna, before 1900] |

| I | 6 | *"Hans im Glück / Eine symphonische Dichtung"* | A.Ms., 1 p., |
| *92* | *E* | Draft for the program of a symphonic poem. Only the beginning of "I. Theil." Note in top right corner, "Motto: 'Ich hab' mein Sach' auf nichts gestellt.'" (The musical sketches for "Hans im Glück" are found with the *Gurre-Lieder* Mss.) | fol., pencil, G., n.p., n.d. [Vienna, ca. 1900] |

| I | 7 | "Symphonische Einleitungsmusik . . ." | A.Ms., 1 p., |
| *92* | *F* | Draft of program for the symphonic poem *Pelleas und Melisande,* op. 5, from 1903. Schoenberg identifies motives that project characters, moods, or ideas from the play. The incomplete draft was eventually crossed out by the composer. | fol., pencil, G., n.p., n.d. [Vienna, ca. 1900] |

| I | 8 | *"Gesang* ([Eduard] Gärtner)" | A.Ms., 1 p., |
| *92* | *G* | Projected, tentative budget for a music education program; includes fees for professional students and dilettantes in 10-month sessions. | fol., ink, G., n.p., n.d. [Vienna, ca. 1900] |

Fragmente

Designation		Subject	Description
II	1	"Gespräch zu zweit, zu dritt . . ." Draft for *Von Heute auf Morgen.* See *Sämtliche Werke,* III/7, 1, p. 15.	A.Ms., 2 p., 4to, pencil, G., n.p., n.d. [late 1928]
II	2	"*Baryton:* Ich suche dich [,] Gott! . . ." Draft for a religious text which treats a theme that recurs in Schoenberg's work beginning with *Die Jakobsleiter:* the paradox that modern man can have faith in spite of an "absent" God. The last line reads: "Und trotzdem glaube ich an dich, denn ich strebe gegen dich."	A.Ms., 1 p., 4to, pencil, G., n.p., n.d. [ca. 1926?]

III 1 *A*   "The Kinds of Construction of a phrase . . ."
Hand- and type-written draft for a textbook on teaching composition. It comprises the following parts:

[p. 1]   The Kinds of construction of a phrase . . .
[p. 2]   I.   [A)] *Repetition of the first phrase* . . .
[p. 3]   I.   B)   Repetition of the first phrase after an interruption . . .
[p. 4]   I.   C   First phrase not at all repeated [not continued]
[p. 5]   II.   What follows the first phrase? . . .
[p. 6]   III.   How are the phrases or parts
         a) connected . . .
         b) joint [*sic*] with one another . . .
[p. 7]   IV.   ANSCHLUSS-TECHNIK
         1. use of contrast
         2. welded together
         3. juxtaposition
         4. joint [*sic*] by use of a remarkable (rhythm or interval) peculiarity of the preceding phrase
         5. up-beat harmonies

Description for III 1 *A*: A.Ms., 2 p., & T. & A.Ms., 5 p., 8vo, ink, E. & G., n.p., n.d. [Brentwood, 1940s]

III 2 *B1*   "Wenn jemand irgend einen Gegenstand . . ."
Sketches and brief notes for essay on the absence of reliable criteria for the evaluation of art, such as those that exist for determining the price of shoes, for instance. Schoenberg suggests: I. quality of thoughts ("Gedankenreichtum"); II. intensity of formulations and thoughts; III. scope of thoughts. He makes an enigmatic reference to Schopenhauer's belief in authoritative

Description for III 2 *B1*: A.Ms., 4 p., 8vo, G. & E., n.p., n.d. [ca. 1927? & 1944?]

Fragmente

Designation		*Subject*	*Description*
		standards. Page 2 begins in German, continues in English with notes on changing fashions in art, on popular music, etc. The draft was perhaps used for the preparation of the lecture "Kriterien musikalischer Werte," 1927 (cf., *SI* 75, p. 518), and, apparently again for the revision of that lecture in 1946. It was again rewritten for publication in *SI* 50, pp. 180-95 ("Criteria for the Evaluation of Music"). See also *SI* 75, pp. 124-36.	
III	3 *B2*	"Criterions of Value in Music" Early version of "Criteria for the Evaluation of Music" (see item 2/*B1,* above). A note in ink reads: "carbon copy under extra copies."	T.Ms. with A.N., 1 p., 4to, E., n.p., n.d. [Brentwood, 1944]
III	4 *C*	"Competition of knowledge . . ." Suggestion for a competition of knowledge of musical literature. Includes details of application and contest procedure, rules, scoring, and prizes.	A.Ms., 4 p., 8vo, pencil, E., n.p., n.d.
III	5 *D*	Set of musical examples for the text on composition, item 1, above: Beethoven, op. 2, no. 1 (first movement and Menuetto), right hand only. The music paper is cut to match the size of item 1.	A.Ms. with musical notation, 2 p., 8vo, ink, n.p., n.d. [Brentwood, 1940s]
IV		The following eleven items are found in one folder; each piece of paper contains a brief, or fragmentary, text. Each page has a number written in pencil in the lower right corner (viz., "7," "34a," etc.). The significance of these numbers has not yet been determined.	
IV	1 7	"beabsichtige: die technischen Mittel . . ." Note concerning the structural principles of various manifestations of "ruhende Bewegung: Das 'Tremolo' / 'Recitativ (?)' / (Waldweben) / Orgelpunkt / am Anfang [, zum] Schluss / und zur Einführung."	A.Ms., 1 p., 16mo, ink, G., n.p., n.d.
IV	2 *34a*	"Die Zeitungen haben es leicht . . ." Critical comment on the ethics of newspapers.	A.Ms., 1 p., obl. 16mo, pencil, G. n.p., n.d.

Fragmente

Designation		Subject	Description
IV	3 *34b*	"Seit dem Beckmesser . . ." Comment on music critics with pun: "Herzerweiterung"—"Gehirnerweichung."	A.Ms., 1 p., 16mo, lilac pencil, G., n.p., n.d.
IV	4 *35a*	"Ein Schurke nennt mich Spekulant . . ." In response to a slur on his integrity, AS creates a fictional situation in which the "scoundrel" takes his best work to court to prove that AS is a swindler. (See FRAGMENTE IV, 9, below.)	A.Ms., 1 p., obl. 16mo, pencil, G., n.p., n.d.
IV	5 *35b*	"Ich scheine wirklich gar nichts von Musik zu verstehen . . ." Schoenberg liked the music of an unidentified composer, but changed his opinion after hearing a remark made by that composer.	A.Ms., 1 p., obl. 16mo, ink, G., n.p., n.d.
IV	6 *37a*	"Clavierstil: . . ." A note about the secret of writing well for the piano.	A.Ms., 1 p., 16mo, pencil, G., n.p., n.d.
IV	7 *37b*	"Wenn man mich fragt . . ." If someone were to ask Schoenberg if all art must have a connection with the past, Schoenberg would answer "no."	A.Ms., 1 p., 16mo, pencil, G., n.p., n.d.
IV	8 *37d*	"Metronom, das Tempo registriert" [Does not continue.]	A.N., 1 p., 16mo, pencil, G., n.p., n.d.
IV	9 *40*	"Es scheint[,] ich habe wirklich . . ." An obscure note in which AS mentions his having robbed a poor devil of some element of style. (See FRAGMENTE IV, 4.)	A.Ms., 1 p., 16mo, ink, G., n.p., n.d.
IV	10 *40a*	"Ich treffe in Berlin . . ." Schoenberg writes a comment about the striking appearance of the people of Berlin.	A.N., 1 p., 16mo, pencil, G., n.p., n.d.
IV	11 *40b*	"Eine Stellung kann nur ehrenvoll sein für einen[,] der sie nicht verdient." Aphorism: A position can only be honorable for the one who does not deserve it.	A.N., 1 p., 16mo, pencil, G., n.p., n.d.

Fragmente

Designation		Subject	Description
V	1	"Do modern composers have ideas? . . ." AS writes an essay about the "critics of modern music" and the difference between teaching and criticism, among other things.	A.Ms., 4 p., 16mo, ink, E., n.p., n.d.
V	2	"Wir wussten, dass wir nicht im Paradies . . ." Before the war (WW I) cultural progress gradually made life more civilized. The war changed that. Doodle in the corner.	A.Ms., 1 p., 16mo, ink, G., n.p., n.d.
V	3	"Es war ein Tag . . ." Casual notes about the rise and fall of France as a great power. At the top of the page: "KFAC 42" (the call letters for an FM radio station in Los Angeles) in pencil, and "Zum Spott / Hohn" in pen. The number "145" is inscribed in a circle. On the left margin: "8 PM," in pencil. Many doodles on the back.	A.Ms., 1 p., 16mo, pencil, G., n.p., n.d.
V	4	"Der Bezugsberechtigte bedingt sich . . ." The title of the piece, "Klausel zum Berechtigungs-vertrag," is written in red pencil following the text. Schoenberg drafts clauses for the protection of authors' right to decide about the transfer of rights, granting of permissions, or changes in works.	A.Ms., 1 p., 8vo, ink, pencil, G., n.p., n.d.
V	5	"Theory of performance (representation) . . ." Schoenberg explains why composers are not as acknowledged as performers are.	A.Ms., 2 p., 8vo, pencil, E., n.p., n.d.
V	6	*"An 12 amerik. Dirigenten"* On the occasion of his 75th birthday (13 September 1949), Schoenberg writes an ironic letter of thanks for the many performances in the previous 15 years during which his works have been neglected. He stipulates that the letter be sent to 12 American conductors and 12 international newspapers. In spite of his lawyer's opinion that the letter is insulting, he will send it, demonstrating his contempt by signing it personally. Draft on the back of program for concert, dated "Thursday, August 18, 1949."	A.L.s., 1 p., 8vo, pencil, G., n.p., [Brentwood, ca. 18 August 1949]
V	7	"Give a savage a *circle* . . ." (in English) This is apparently an outline for a presentation; it comprises a series of ideas in loosely-connected order. AS begins with a comparison of the behavior of a "savage"	A.Ms., 1 p., 8vo, pencil, E. & G., n.p., n.d.

Fragmente

Designation		Subject	Description
		and his friend "R." when given a circle, and continues on to the following ideas with no particular development: the variety of means in musical logic (example: *Kammersymphonie*); the consolidation of logic by the 12-tone technique; the necessity for a system to emerge from (extant) works; his support for learning basic skills.	
V	8	"Musical notation is done in rebusses . . ." Notes written on an unfolded envelope which is addressed to the Schoenbergs at their Brentwood residence; the stamp cancellation reads "Los Angeles/Mar 15/1945." The ideas concern the changing concepts of loudness and balance between the orchestra and soloists since Bach, with examples from Weber (*Der Freischütz*), Beethoven (*Fidelio*) and Wagner, where soloists are covered. Other notes mention the conductor's role in clarifying the score and the performance of dotted notes "quasi legato."	A.N., 2 p., 8vo, pencil, E., Los Angeles [Brentwood], n.d. [ca. 15 March 1945]
V	9	"Herr Rufer hatte das Recht . . ." Draft for a letter written on an unfolded envelope, apparently to the Kroll-Oper, Berlin. Schoenberg explains that Rufer had the authority to negotiate the rights for the first performance of V[on] H[eute] a[uf] M[orgen]. The Intendant of the Kroll Opera did not answer AS's letters, and, in addition, [Otto] Klemperer declared the score to be the hardest he had seen. So, AS gave the rights to Josef Turnan, Intendant of the opera in Frankfurt.	A.L., 1 p., 8vo, pencil & ink, G., n.p., n.d. [Berlin?, 1929]
VI	1	"Ältere Satzbaukunst: . . ." Schoenberg is first concerned with the symmetry and unity of elements in the music of Haydn, Mozart, and Beethoven. In contrast the music of Mahler uses either a strict 4- or 2-meter, or rhythmic freedom, "(Prosa??)." Mozart's interpunctuation is more diversified than Mahler's because the former uses measures larger than his motifs while the latter's motifs are longer than his measures.	A.Ms., 2 p., 8vo, ink, G., n.p., n.d.
VI	2	"Strauss / 'Wenn man dem Publikum . . .'" Satiric comment on Richard Strauss' cynical remarks about his audiences. AS compares Strauss ("unserer berühmtester Hofkonditor"), who hides problems behind a layer of frosting, to Mahler, in whose symphonies form is commensurate with content.	A.Ms., 4 p., 16mo, ink, G., n.p., n.d.

Fragmente

Designation		Subject	Description
VI	3	"Article about [Adolph] Loos:" AS notes down ideas which include his view of sculpture and his explanation of the effect of photography on painting. A blue line on the left side of the sheet indicates that the item could belong to BIOGRAPHISCHES II, above.	A.Ms., 1 p., 8vo, pencil, E., n.p., n.d. [Los Angeles, ca. 1944]
VI	4	"freut mich / dass es nicht . . ." Draft for letter with the salutation "Sehr geehrte Herren," a reply to a supportive letter AS received while in Barcelona. The item has some doodles.	A.L., 1 p., 8vo, ink, G., n.p., n.d. [Barcelona, late 1931]
VI	5	"Leider nicht von Johs. Brahms" Schoenberg at play: a "forgery" of Brahms' signature together with 4 measures of (Strauss') "An der schönen blauen Donau," and 4 measures of Brahms' *Piano Quartet,* op. 25, with the inscription "leider von Johannes Brahms / only orchestrated by Arnold Schoenberg" (German and English).	A.N., 1 p., 8vo, ink, G. & E., n.p., n.d.

Kleine Manuskripte

Designation		Subject	Description
I C-29		A collection of disparate Mss., some of which are stapled, glued or bound together in groups of 2 or 3, though they apparently have nothing in common.	
I C-29	1 cover	*"KLEINE MANUSKRIPTE I"* Self-made cover of cardboard and heavy paper reinforced with tape on left side for binding with brads. "C-29" is written in red pencil; "29" in green; "KLEINE MANUSKRIPTE I" in black crayon pencil. A carbon copy of a typed table of contents is pasted onto the front:	

A page from Schoenberg's own catalog of manuscripts showing the numbers, categories, titles and dates of origin of items listed. Note numbers 84 and 125 found in illustrations elsewhere in this volume.

Kleine Manuskripte

Designation	*Subject*	*Description*

Vorwort zu Webern's Liedern
An einen Musikkritiker
Für echt niederländische Künste
  (weiter hinten 2. Blätt)
Zum Mendelssohn-Preis
Casella's Musik
An einen "Freund"
12-Tonschrift
Aphorismus: Teilnahmslosigkeit
1. Versuch zu "Neuer Klassizismus"
Fragen v. Jens. Qu. - - Der Dirigent
Mendelssohn[-] Preis

The table of contents was apparently prepared in America. The "29" in the designation "C-29" refers to Schoenberg's Ms. List B: "29, Kleine Manuskripte I / Inhalt siehe spezielle Listen." An addendum to that list contains a typed copy of the above table of contents.

Designation	Subject	Description
I C-29 2	"So sehr für diese Stücke . . ." Typewritten draft for the preface to Webern's *Bagatelles,* which Schoenberg calls "Lieder" in the above table of contents. See *Sechs Bagatellen,* op. 9 (Vienna: Universal Edition, 1924), p. 2. A translation is found in *SI* 75, pp. 483-84.	T.Ms. with A.N. in ink, 1 p., 8vo, G., n.p., n.d. [Mödling, 1924]
I C-29 3 366 367	"Da ich in . . . Ihrem Blatt . . ." One of two items (nos. 3 and 4) stapled together. Draft for a reply to the editor of an unidentified journal in which AS suggests that he look in published reference books for the biographical information he requested. AS also mentions unfriendly treatment on the part of the journal. The significance of the numbers "366" (stamped once) and "367" (stamped three times) has not been determined.	A.L., 1 p., 16mo, ink, G., n.p., n.d.
I C-29 4 392 393	"Das ganze zu greifen . . ." Draft for a review of an (unidentified) music theory text. AS criticizes the author's ignorance, lack of taste, old-fashioned examples, among other things. He also comments that the editor's interpolations merely serve to make the reprint more expensive. The numbers "392" and "393" have not been identified. This item was stapled to item 3, above.	A.Ms., 2 p., 16mo, ink, G., n.p., n.d.

Kleine Manuskripte

Designation		Subject	Description
I C-29	5	**"Gebouw niederländischer Kunst . . ."** The first of two Mss. bound together (nos. 5 and 9). It contains brief sketches for the dedication of the Concertgebouw canon. The last sketch, "Für echt niederländische Künste . . . ," is close to the final version printed in facsimile in Rufer, *Work,* facing p. 88.	A.Ms.s., 1 p., 8vo, pencil, G., n.p., n.d., [Berlin, 1928]
I C-29	6	**"Es ist mir eine Freude . . ."** Schoenberg drafted his greeting to the Concertgebouw Orchestra and its conductor Mengelberg, on the back of a letter addressed to him from Jac. M. Goedemans. It was AS's response to Goedemans' request for a short article for the Amsterdam *Telegraaf* on the occasion of the jubilee celebration of the orchestra's 40th year. Apparently, "weiter hinten 2. Blatt" in the above table of contents refers to this item.	A.N., 1 p., 8vo, G., [Berlin, 1928], written on T.L., 1 p., 8vo, G., *16. Marz 1928*
I C-29	7	**"Sehr verehrter Herr Professor!"** A letter, signed "Schünemann," addressed to Schoenberg from the Director of the Staatl.[iche] akad.[emische] Hochschule für Musik in Berlin. It provides information about Klaus Langer who studied composition with Profs. [Franz] Schreker and [Paul] Juon. The information was apparently sent to AS in connection with his position as a judge in the Mendelssohn-Bartholdy competition. The item was stapled to item 16, below, which concerns the competition.	T.L. [to Schoenberg], 1 p., 8vo, G., *Berlin, 6. September 1932*
I C-29	8	**"1. / Hannenheim, Norbert / Meisterschule . . ."** A sheet of music paper with extensive comments on works by student composers being considered for the Mendelssohn prize for composition. AS listed participants' names, ages, schools, and teachers, and noted his first impression of works as well as his final evaluation. Four students from his own master-class participated: Norbert Hannenheim, Peter Schacht, Nikolas Skalkottas, and Bernd Bergel. Others were Hans Norbert [or Karl?] Langer, August Karl Kreussler, Heinz Panels, Karl Höller, Harald Genzmer, Adolf Fecker, H. Spittler, and Jedig [?] Arbahty. Schoenberg wanted additional information on Langer (see item 7, above). The item has some music notations. It was stapled together with item 7.	A.D., 1 p., fol., pencil & ink, G., n.p., n.d. [Berlin, 1932]

Kleine Manuskripte

Designation		Subject	Description
I C-29	9	"you can perhaps note a significant independence . . ." The second of two Mss. bound together (items 5 and 9). Notes about Alfredo Casella, mostly in English. One note, in German, reads: "schnelle Noten / schnell reden / damit das Publikum keine Zeit hat nachzudenken / Dann ein happy end," followed by a notation of a C-major chord. Two short musical examples illustrate remarks about tonality vs. atonality. The final articulation of these ideas is found in the unpublished article "Fascism Is No Article for Exportation," written in 1935 in response to Casella's writings. (See *Schriften,* pp. 313-19, where it is published in German translation.)	A.Ms., 2 p., 8vo, ink & pencil, E. & G., n.p., n.d. [Hollywood, 1935]
I C-29	10	"Nach mir so l das h bennannt werden . . ." One of three small sheets which are glued together forming an assemblage. This item and 12, below, are glued to the right side and bottom of item 11, below. The content of item 10 is a cryptic typed note, as above, together with a handwritten note: "zur 12 Ton Notenschrift." The connection between this designation and the contents of the three sheets is difficult to make. (See AS's article, "Eine neue Zwölfton-Schrift," from 1924, published in *Schriften,* pp. 198-205, and in translation in *SI* 75, pp. 354ff.)	T.N. with A.N.s., 1 p., 16mo, n.p., n.d. [ca. 1924]
I C-29	11	"Die Universität i zu mitieren . . ." This item is a torn page from an appointment calendar on the back of which AS typed a 4-line rhymed poem composed in a simple code ("i zu mitieren" = "zu imitieren"). It makes fun of music teachers with academic pretensions. This apparently refers to events in connection with the change of the name of the Music Academy in Vienna from "Akademie" to "Hochschule." (See Schoenberg's comments in his "Meine Nichtberufung," BIOGRAPHISCHES III, 3.)	T.Ms., 1 p., 16mo, G., n.p., n.d. [ca. 1923]
I C-29	12	"Sehr geehrter Herr . . ." Glued to item 10, above, we find this handwritten draft for a thank-you letter to an unidentified person who had apparently returned a borrowed letter to AS. The message is difficult to decipher and has numerous corrections, insertions, deletions.	A.L., 1 p., 16mo, ink, G., n.p., n.d.

Kleine Manuskripte

Designation		Subject	Description
I C-29	13	"Teilnahmslosigkeit ist die primitivste Form des Widerstandes . . ." Draft for a letter to an unidentified person. In aphoristic terms AS states his support of efforts to help persons with little money attend music performances.	A.L., 1 p., 8vo, ink, G., n.p., n.d.
I C-29	14	"Vorsänger: Ich habs [*sic*] . . ." Draft for the text for the little cantata *Der neue Klassizismus,* published in *Drei Satiren,* op. 28, in 1926. The cantata was written at the end of 1925; the date on the Ms. "13/II. 1926," is problematic.	A.Ms., 1 p., obl. 16mo, ink, G., n.p. [Berlin], *13/II. 1926*
I C-29	15	"Fragen von J. Qu. . . ." Typed manuscript for a note in *Pult und Taktstock.* (See JENS. QUER., 2, below.)	T.N., large 8vo, G., n.p., n.d., [1924?]
I C-29	16	"1932 / Bewerber . . ." AS's notes for his evaluation of the applicants for the Mendelssohn-Bartholdy Prize for performers. He lists names of participants and relevant details of qualification as well as brief comments on a few performances. Many doodles and a music notation: 3 measures of the main theme of Brahms' Violin Concerto.	A.N., 1 p., fol., ink, G., n.p. [Berlin], *1932*
II C-30	1 Cover	"Kleine Manuskripte II" Self-made cardboard folder. Pasted onto front page is the following typed table of contents. Schoenberg indicates the number of pages in each item in the parentheses. Aphorisms (2) Die heutige Jugend (1) Louis ist Kritiker [no page numbers indicated] Die Kultur hat die Tendenz (1) Vortrag: Breslau Glückl.[iche] Hand (3) Schutzbund f.[ür] Geistige Kultur (1) Die mir die Nachwelt geraubt (1) Ich habe über Gustav Mahler (1) . . . gewissenlose Spekulanten . . . (1) Werke der Tonkunst werden heute mangels (1) a) Vorwort zu op. 22, handschr[iftlich] (2) b) Vorwort zu op. 22, maschin[enschriftlich] Ich sehe mit Schrecken, dass Sevcik (1)	A.D., 1 p., fol., pencil; with T.D., 1 p., 16mo, carbon, G. & E., n.p., n.d. [after 1933]

Kleine Manuskripte

Designation		Subject	Description

Designation   *Subject*   *Description*

The contents of the collection correspond to the above table with the one exception that the typed preface to op. 22 (item 14, below) lacks the last two pages. The number "30" indicates the location of the collection on Ms. List B: 30, "Kleine Manuskripte II." An additional comment, "Inhalt siehe spezielle Listen," refers to the addendum to this list which contains a copy of the typed table of contents above. Details of the language indicate that the cover was prepared during the American years.

II   C-30   2   *"Aphorismen"*
Draft for a collection of aphorisms with many deletions and corrections. The contents are as follows:

> Dass der Raubmörder . . . / Frauen sind ehrgeizig . . . / Meine Sache ist meine Person . . . / Der Künstler kann viel weniger . . . / An die einträglichen Stellen . . . / Leute, die mich aufsuchen . . . / Welcher Art der Unterschied zwischen Talent und Genie ist . . . / Ich bin dafür, dass man statt "Talent" . . . / Karl Kraus' Wort: Das Gehirnweichbild Wiens . . . / Er sah mich dabei vielsagend an . . . / Der Kritiker bringt es nicht über sich . . . / Das Porträt hat nicht dem Modell . . . / Man lernts [*sic*]: jetzt kann ich schon . . . / Der Künstler hat nie ein Verhältnis zur Welt . . ."

The same collection was printed in *Gutmanns Konzert-Kalender,* 1911/12. (See APHORISMEN VII, 2, below.)

Description: A.Ms., 2 p., 8vo, pencil & ink, G., n.p., n.d. [ca. 1911]

II   C-30   3   "Die heutige Jugend . . ."
A lengthy commentary in which Schoenberg expresses his opinion that the revolution in art is only apparent; creativity comes from the same source now as earlier. (A duplicate is found in APHORISMEN I, 56 with the tentative date "April 1931." A variant of the text is found in DICHTUNGEN 4g, below.)

Description: T.Ms., 1 p., 4to, carbon, G., n.p., n.d. [Berlin, 1931]

II   C-30   4   "Aber Louis ist Kritiker"
A music critic named Louis (the Munich critic, Rudolf Louis?) attacks composers, particularly Jewish composers, without reason. He then seeks shelter behind the music critics' guild, the "Plattenbrüderschaft."

Description: A.Ms., 1 p., 4to, pencil, G., n.p., n.d.

Kleine Manuskripte

Designation		Subject	Description
II C-30	5	"Die Kultur hat unter anderem die Tendenz . . ." In this unfinished essay, marked with many corrections and deletions, Schoenberg states his belief in the benefits of culture which accrue slowly, but which serve to temper the elementary and wild instincts of people.	A.Ms., 1 p., 4to, ink, G., n.p., n.d.
II C-30	6	"Hat es Sinn, dass ein Autor . . ." Outline for a lecture at Breslau on the occasion of the 1928 production of *Die glückliche Hand*. It deviates considerably from the final speech published in *Schriften*, pp. 235-39. The page is stamped twice with Schoenberg's Nussbaum-Allee address. The draft is written on the back of a printed formal thank-you letter on the occasion of AS's 50th birthday. This page is dated "Oktober 1924."	A.Ms., 1 p., 4to, pencil, G., *Char-lottenburg*, [Berlin], n.d. [1928]
II C-30	7	"Meine verehrten Damen und Herren / Ich befinde mich . . ." This piece is an elaboration of the first point in the draft (item 6, above) about the author's right to explain his own creations. It was evidently rejected as the introduction to the speech. Page 2 is stamped 3 times with Schoenberg's name and the Kantstrasse address.	A.Ms., 2 p., 4to, pencil, G., Char-lottenburg [Berlin], n.d. [1928]
II C-30	8	*"Schutzbund für geistige Kultur"* Prospectus for an organization which would serve to protect intellectual culture. Lays down basic principles and creates categories of membership. Translated into English in Christensen, "Developing the Good Instincts," *Sinfonian* 32, no. 3 (1983). (AS mentions this project in a letter to Alban Berg of 2 January 1935. See Stuckenschmidt, *Schoenberg,* p. 542f.)	A.Ms., 1 p., 4to, ink, G., n.p. [Hollywood], *1. Jänner 1935*
II C-30	9	"Die mir die Mitwelt geraubt" A poem of 8 lines with several corrections and deletions. It concerns the concepts of fame and integrity. A note, associated with a drawing of steps reads "Darf ich eintreten / Du tritts [*sic*] ein / B. Es. E. A." The item has a doodle in the corner; the front is stamped with AS's Canyon Cove address and signed in printed lettering.	A.Ms. with A.N.s., 1 p., 4to, ink, Hollywood, n.d. [ca. 1935]

Kleine Manuskripte

Designation		Subject	Description
II C-30	10	"Ich habe über Gustav Mahler nicht viel zu sagen . . ." Draft for a laudatory essay on Mahler in which AS writes that Mahler is one of the greatest persons of all times. Schoenberg is convinced of a new development in aesthetics in response to Mahler's works. The draft apparently predates Mahler's death on 18 May 1911, but the opening lines evoke the beginning of the lecture "Gustav Mahler: in memoriam," from 1912. (See *SI* 75, pp. 449ff.)	A.Ms., 1 p., 4to, pencil, G., n.p., n.d.
II C-30	11	"In einem Referat über ein Kompositionskonzert . . ." Schoenberg responds to a phrase, "gewissenlosen Spekulanten," used by the critic Paul Stauber in the *Extrablatt* from 26 April 1911, to characterize a concert which included a work by Schoenberg. He challenges Stauber to specify that the phrase refers to him. If Stauber replies in the affirmative, Schoenberg threatens to sue him for libel.	A.L.s., 1 p., fol., pencil, G., n.p. [Vienna], *26. April 1911*
II C-30	12	"Werke der Tonkunst werden heute . . ." Schoenberg comments on the present-day tendency to consider compositions only with respect to the performer.	T.Ms., 1 p., 4to, G., n.p., n.d.
II C-30	13	"Nach langem Zögern habe ich . . ." Heavily revised and corrected draft for an article, item 14, below. Each page is stamped with the composer's name and the Gloriettegasse address.	A.Ms., 4 p., 8vo, and 1 p., fol., ink & pencil, G., *Wien*, n.d. [1917]
II C-30	13 Cover	"Als Vorwort zu den 4 Orch.[ester] Liedern, Op. 22, 1-4" Title page for the Ms., item 13. Stamped with Schoenberg's name and Gloriettegasse address.	A.D., 1 p., fol., G., *Wien*, n.d. [1917]
II C-30	14	"Die vereinfachte Studier- und Dirigier-Partitur" Typed Ms. with some substantial revisions. Each page stamped with Schoenberg's name and the Gloriettegasse address. The article was published as the preface of the *Vier Orchesterlieder*, op. 22 (Vienna: Universal Edition, 1917), pp. 2-3. See *Schriften*, pp. 179-81.	T.Ms. with A.N., 4 p., fol., ink, G., *Wien*, n.d. [1917]

Kleine Manuskripte

Designation		Subject	Description

| II
C-30 | 15 | "Ich sehe mit Schrecken, dass Sevcik . . ." AS's notations for spiccato and staccato differs from Ševčik's. Schoenberg traces his own signs to Leopold Mozart's *Violinschule*. In an added note AS mentions that his practice has been consistent since the *Serenade,* op. 24. | T.Ms., 1 p., fol., G., *Mödling, 30. Mai 1923;* T.N., G., *Traunkirchen, 25. Juni 1925* |
| III
7 | 1
Cover | "Kleine Manuskripte 7" Purchased hard paper binding which contained the 12 items, below (A-M). The title and the number ("7," inscribed in a circle) are in black crayon pencil; "A-M" is in green pencil. Glued to the front is a 16mo sheet with the table of contents typewritten as follows: | T. & A.D., 1 p., 8vo, pencil, n.p., n.d. [Los Angeles, after 1934] |

> A) 1, 2, 3. Text zu einem Chor
> B) Vormerkungen für zu schreibende Glossen, etc.
> C) Glossen in Heyse's Grammatik
> D) Kunst nicht revolutionär
> E) Triolen und Quartolen bei Brahms und Bach
> F) Aphorismus: Butter auf den (dem) Kopf
> G) Entwurf (Fragment) Vortrag Princeton Melody
>   and Harmony (9)
> H) Meine Kanons (unvollständig)
> I) Vorschlag an Furtwängler (2)
> K) Weihnachten 1930 (neuer Schreibtisch)
> L) Konstruierte Musik (4 pages, 2 sheets)
> M) Schüleraufnahme (Malkin Conservatory)

Table and title date post March 1934, the period of the Princeton lecture. The relevance of the number "7" has yet to be determined.

| III
7 | 2a
A1 | "Text zu einem Chor" The text for a choral work beginning "Der Mensch ist bös. . . ." "Abschrift" written in top right corner indicates that the item is a copy of an aphorism from 1931. (See APHORISMEN I, 41.) Both the aphorism and the present text contain notes indicating AS's decision to compose a counter-strophe beginning "Der Mensch ist gut!" | A.Ms., 1 p., 8vo, ink, G., *Territet oder Barcelona, 1931?,* [Berlin, 1932] |
| III
7 | 2b
A2 | "Er folgt nicht sklavisch . . ." The second strophe of the choral text arranged in 5 paired lines, each pair with letter identification. Continued with draft for third strophe: "Man begreift es nicht . . ." in | A.Ms., 1 p., 8vo, ink, G., n.p., n.d. |

Kleine Manuskripte

Designation		Subject	Description
		which Schoenberg poses the question about the growth of evil from innocence. (The first and second strophe are rendered in translation in Christensen, "Spiritual and Material," *Music and Letters* 65, no. 4 [October 1984]: 339.)	[Berlin, 1932]
III *7*	2c *A3*	"Der Mensch ist gut!" Schematic arrangement of the lines of the second strophe with revised identifications of line pairs. Text partially rewritten. Some doodles.	A.Ms., 1 p., 8vo, n.p. [Berlin], *10/X. 1932*
III *7*	3 *B*	*"Anekdoten: Busoni . . ."* Collection of fragmentary anecdotes, most of which are about musicians. One of several about Busoni mentions his lack of response to AS's plan for peace based on Kaiser Karl and Wilson's 14 Points which AS had circulated. Other anecdotes refer to [Franz] Schalk, Siegfried Ochs (concerns the rehearsals of *Gurre-Lieder*), and Paul Stefan (who had a mysterious ability to be two places at once). For fun, he ranks waiters, servants, nurses, horn players, and composers as members of the international swindler's school ("Die Internationale Gaunerschule").	A.Ms., 2 p., 8vo, ink, G., n.p., n.d.
III *7*	4 *C*	"In Heyses Deutscher Grammatik einige längere Ausführungen." (Complete as is.)	A.N., 1 p., 8vo, black crayon pencil, G., n.p., n.d.
III *7*	5 *D*	"verschiedene Ausdrücke:" Essay on the common idea that art is revolutionary. Schoenberg disagrees: after 50 years that which once seemed revolutionary is viewed as having been a consequent development.	A.Ms., 1 p., 8vo, pencil, n.p., n.d.
III *7*	6 *E*	"Als Beweis, dass die Behauptung . . ." Comment on the interpretation of triplets and quadruplets. He illustrates with musical quotes from Brahms' "An den Mond," op. 71, no. 2, and his B♭ major String Quartet, op. 67, and from Bach's *St. Matthew Passion.* Written on pages 23 and 24 of a small purchased notebook.	A.Ms., 2 p., 8vo, ink, G., *26. VI.1934* *27. VI.1934*

Kleine Manuskripte

Designation		Subject	Description
III 7	7 F	"Butter ist in diesem Land . . ." Aphoristic comment about America. Written on page 25 of a small purchased notebook.	A.Ms., 1 p., 8vo, ink, G., n.p. [Hollywood], *November, 1934*
III 7	8 G	"Harm[onie] u[nd] Mel[odie] / Entwurf [/] Vortrag für Princeton" Draft for a lecture planned for Princeton University in early 1934. On p. 1, AS indicates a title, "Glossen über das Verhältnis zwischen Harmonie und Melodie," which he translates into English: "From the relation (connection) between melody and harmony." The speech is incomplete; a portion is in final draft form and the rest is outlined. Musical examples are partially incorporated into the text. Schoenberg maintains that the harmony of "primitive" (pentatonic) melodies, folksongs, and chorales is implicitly present in the melody, and that "art" music, which is based on variation, brings out the rich harmonic potential inherent in melody ("ein Mehr an Harmonie"). He takes examples from his own early works, in particular *Gurre-Lieder* and the *Kammersymphonie,* op. 9. On p. 9, he points out that the melody of an example from the latter work demonstrates greater harmonic innovation than does the harmony. A note (p. 8), dated *Ende December 1934* (actually 1933), documents his decision to change the topic of his lecture to 12-tone composition. (For a discussion of that lecture, see C. Spies, "Vortrag," *Perspectives of New Music* 13 [1974]: 58-136.)	A.Ms., 9 p., 8vo, ink, G. & E., n.p. [Hollywood] *Ende December 1934* [December. 1933]
III 7	9 H	"Kanons etc" Incomplete list of AS's canons: 　　Kanon f.[ür] G.[esellschaft] D.[eutscher] 　　　　　　　T[onkünstler] 　　　　*"　　　"* 　Concertgeb.[ouw] 　　　　*"　　　"* 　D. Wolfsohn 　　　　*"　　　"* 　Abraham 　　　　*"　　　"* 　Streichquartett	A.N., 1 p., 8vo, pencil, G., n.p., n.d. [after 1934]
III 7	10 I	"VORSCHLAG / An Furtwängler:" Draft for a letter to the conductor in which AS requests Furtwängler's assistance in promoting his plan for the establishment of a Jewish state. The letter outlines a plan	A.L., 2 p., 8vo, ink, G., n.p., n.d. [1933?]

Kleine Manuskripte

Designation		Subject	Description
		to reconcile Jewish and German views. The two pages of the Ms. are glued to a protective sheet of brown paper.	
III	11	"Weihnachten 1930, an einem neuen Schreibtisch . . ." AS pens an epigrammatic seasonal greeting. On the reverse: a short unidentified musical notation; AS's name carefully printed; and his Nürnberger Platz address stamped 6 times. The 16mo sheet is glued to an 8vo sheet of brown paper. The letter "K" appears on the brown paper cover of the preceding item (10, above), which covered the smaller one in question in the folder.	A.N.s., 2 p̓., 16mo, ink, G., *Berlin, Weihnachten 1930*
7	K		
III	12	*"Konstruktierte [sic] Musik"* Draft for an article containing a calm assessment of the relationship between musical composition and construction. The finished article is published in *SI* 75, pp. 106-08, as "Constructed Music." The sheets are attached to oblong 16mo pieces of stiff paper. The curious spelling "Konstruktierte" in the title is not repeated in the text. (See DICHTUNGEN 4a, and APHORISMEN I, 31 and 57.)	A.Ms., 4 p., 8vo, ink, G., n.p., n.d.
7	L		
III	13	"Schüleraufnahme für dieses Semester . . ." Assessment of American students after becoming acquainted with the situation at the Malkin Conservatory following registration for the semester. Schoenberg finds as many good teachers and students in America as in Europe, and, perhaps a more positive attitude. On the negative side: students finish schooling too soon due to lack of funding; that is, 3 to 4 years instead of 6 to 10, as needed. AS reiterates his belief in education, regardless of whether it produces great masters or not.	A.Ms., 2 p., 8vo, ink, G., n.p., n.d. [Boston, ca. 1934]
7	M		

Sprachliches

Designation	Subject	Description
	A collection of Mss. devoted to commentary on the use and abuse of various idioms.	

Sprachliches

Designation	Subject	Description
1 *SPR* *215 a-k*	Six pages bound together with a strip of brown paper on the left side. "SPR a-c" have no common heading; "SPR d-f" treat "Sprache der Reklame"; "SPR i-k" comment on the language of music critics. Each subject is identified by a letter and is dated individually:	A.Ms.s., 6 p., 8vo, ink, G., n.p. [Berlin], *29.V.1927 - 6/IV - 1929*

	1 *a* *"Aberhundert-Abertausend"*	*29.V.1927*
	1 *b* *"Das ist nicht gesagt"*	*23.VI.1927*
	1 *c* *"Derselbe"*	*3/VII. 1927*
	1 *d-f* *"Sprache der Reklame:"* "Staunend billige Preise" *"Qualitätsware"* *"Sieben billige Handschuhtage"*	*5.IX.1927*
	1 *g* *"Die Deutschesten"* National Socialist propaganda language: "aufmöbeln" was coined to avoid the communist slogan "aufputschen."	*25/V. 1928*
	1 *h* *"Tennis-Sprache"* AS suggests improvements in German translations of English tennis terms such as "Flugball," "Hochball," etc.	*25.V.1928*
	1 *i* *"Karpath* müsste von mir wieder sagen . . ." AS comments on a self-contradictory statement made by the Viennese critic more than 20 years earlier.	*3/4. 1929*
	1 *k* *"Weissmann—*Der konnte hier oft auftreten . . ." AS ridicules the Berlin critic's characterization of him as an "substanzarmer Eigenbrötler der Musik."	*6/IV. 1929*

Note: AS omitted "j" as an identifying letter in the above list.

| 2
SPR
370 | " --- *angenehm enttäuscht* ---- "
In a 3-month period (September-November 1932), Schoenberg makes a series of observations about misuse of language. He generally cites the offending construction (e.g., *"keine Lorbeeren gepflückt," "gehobene Stände," "Peinlicher Prozess für H."*) and makes an analytic comment about them. In one comment he asserts that these mistakes are the result of an educational program which aims at creating a 20,000 word vocabulary, while most persons are capable of using only 4,000 words. | A.Ms., 2 p., 8vo, ink, G., n.p. [Berlin], *28.IX.1932, 8/X. 1932, 19.XI.1932* |

Dichtungen, Texte, Sprüche, Aphorismen

Designation	Subject	Description
1 Cover	"List of Writings" Schoenberg devised a title page for a collection of texts and for lists of texts of his literary works. As indicated by the heading, the collection is mixed, though all are of a "poetic" character as opposed to essays, for example. Some are published, others are not. The table of contents reads:	T.D., 1 p., 4to, G. & E., n.p., n.d. [Brentwood, ca. 1947]

> List of Writings
> Stücke, men's voices, op. 35
>   Six Männerchöre, Texte   pp. 1-3
> Aphorismen, Anekdoten, Sprüche
>   Aph. Anek.   pp. 1-14
> Stücke, mixed voices, op. 27
>   Gemischte Chöre, Texte
> Satiren
>   3 Satiren, Texte
> [Canons]
>   Canons, Texte zu Kanons

This collection apparently was intended to be a record of all Schoenberg's writings in a typed original and three copies. There are actually only a number of the shorter texts and one comprehensive collection of aphorisms, while a portion of the remaining work is named on a list (also in an original and three carbon copies). In the sub-group "Texte" (5, below) the text for *A Survivor from Warsaw* is represented by three copies, although it does not appear in the list of writings, and *Israel Exists Again* is listed but not represented. In the group of texts for canons (6, below) many texts are listed but not included. An estimate of the total number of pages of the planned collection is found elsewhere (see APHORISMEN III, 1).

Designation	Subject	Description
2.1-4	"Dichtungen, Texte, Sprüche, Aphorismen" Original and three copies of a list of AS's texts for his larger vocal works.	T.D., 1 p., 4to, n.p., n.d. [1940s]
3.1-4	"6 Männer-Chöre" Original and three copies of the following texts: "Hemmung," "Das Gesetz," "Ausdrucksweise," "Glück," "Landsknechte," "Verbundenheit."	T.Ms., 3 p., 4to, G., n.p., n.d. [1940s]

Dichtungen, Texte, Sprüche, Aphorismen

Designation	*Subject*	*Description*
4.1-4 *APH /* *ANEK*	"APHORISMEN, ANEKDOTEN, SPRUECHE" A collection of 36 aphorisms, several of which are extensive, prepared from the autograph Ms. APHORISMEN III, 2, but arranged in a different order. The dates for the individual aphorisms are taken from the A.Ms., and indicate the year of composition. The abbreviated heading "Aph./Anek." is typed on the upper right corner of each page, beginning with page 2. Page 3 is headed *"APHORISMS"* and the page set-up from this page to the end differs from pp. 1-2. AS has indicated that item 4dd needs to be re-written. The collection includes the following aphorisms in original and copies:	T.Ms., 14 p., 4to, G. & E., n.p. [Brentwood], *1949*
4a	"Wenige wissen heute . . ." Paraphrasing the term "norddeutsche Verstandesmusik," AS calls himself a "süddeutscher Konstrukteur." (Variant of APHORISMEN III, 2, dated 1927. See APHORISMEN I, 31 and 57.)	n.d. [1927]
4b	"Ich habe es immer verwunderlich gefunden, . . ." Why are badly-tuned triads acceptable and major sevenths inacceptable? (See APHORISMEN I, 57.)	n.d.
4c	"In meiner Jugend . . ." In Schoenberg's youth snobs called difficult music "interesting." (See APHORISMEN I, 57.)	n.d.
4d	*"Opernkrise* / Es heisst, die Oper befinde sich . . ." Opera tends to be overwhelmed by theatrical accessories. Gustav Mahler took control of the situation. This essay is published in *Anbruch* 8/5 (1926): 209, with the title: "Gibt es eine Krise der Oper?" (See APHORISMEN I, 57.)	n.d. [1926]
4e	"Wenn fünf Menschen und ein Affe . . ." Aphorism about mimicry, inspired by an event AS read about in a music journal in 1936. It was reported that a music professor in Boston imitated the style of AS's "Five Piano Pieces, op. 10" (a mistake which AS comments on), and "fooled" a group of music teachers. (See APHORISMEN I, 48.)	n.d. [1936]

Dichtungen, Texte, Sprüche, Aphorismen

Designation	Subject	Description
4f	"Die Nähe – zeitlich – verdunkelt . . ." Short essay on the relativity of music history. Contemporary issues are of revolutionary importance while the revolutions of the past are indistinct commonplaces (e.g., Mozart's harmonic advances). The conclusion was rewritten in 1949: Schoenberg imagines that Le[ver]kühn will some day be named the inventor of the 12-tone method.	*1932, 1949*
4g	"Es gibt nur einen direkten Weg . . ." Concerns tradition. (Variant of KLEINE MANUSKRIPTE II. 3, above.)	n.d.
4h	"Musiker ist einer . . ." Schoenberg makes a distinction between a musician and an instrumentalist.	n.d.
4i	"Das Vibrato hat man in meiner Jugend . . ." Extended essay on the use of vibrato. Published in English translation in *SI* 75, "Vibrato," pp. 345-47, and dated "around 1940."	n.d.[ca. 1940]
4j	"Warum tragen Boxer, Fussballer, Tennisspieler u.a. nicht Frack . . ." Essay inspired by the contrast between the uniforms of the performers of past eras and those of today, and between the great patrons before 1800 – Friedrich der Grosse, Emperor Joseph II – and "Ihre Majestät das Publikum" today. (See NOTEBOOKS II, 1, below.)	n.d.
4k	"'. . . tonality in music, as realism in painting . . .'" A comment on an unidentified book about music (*Music Ho!* by Constance Lambert, see APHORISMEN I, 55). AS takes issue with the author's view that tonality and realism are dictated by our blood.	*1934*
4l	"Man sollte nicht verächtlich von Erfolgen sprechen . . ." Good luck is a sign of the chosen ones. (Variant of APHORISMEN I, 49a.)	*1929*
4m	"*Ich als Nero* / Wenn diese drei Kritiker . . ." A very short aphorism in which AS comments that if three particular but unidentified critics had *one* head between them, he wouldn't have to chop it off. (See APHORISMEN I, 49b.)	*1929*

Dichtungen, Texte, Sprüche, Aphorismen

Designation	Subject	Description
4n	"Manche Behauptung . . ." Concerns the confusion of language when it comes to making clear postulates. (See APHORISMEN I, 47.)	n.d.
4o	"Abkömmlinge von meiner Musik . . . / Alle diese haben zuerst etwas aus mir gemacht!" AS comments on the partisans of his music. (Variant of APHORISMEN I, 39.)	*1928*
4p	"Meine Originalität kommt daher . . ." The source of Schoenberg's originality according to himself is that he imitates everything — including things he has never seen before. (Variant of APHORISMEN I, 30a.)	*1925*
4q	"Andere Abkömmlinge von mir: / meine Wünsche gehen . . . in Erfüllung . . ." Schoenberg desires to have as few followers as possible. (Variant of APHORISMEN I, 30b.)	*1925*
4r	"*Internationale Kriecher* / Die internationalen Feste für neue Musik . . ." Schoenberg is concerned with the communication between creators and critics during music festivals. (Variant of APHORISMEN I, 27.)	*1926*
4s	"Meinen ehemaligen Mitläufern . . ." Schoenberg comments on his followers in the past. (Variant of APHORISMEN I, 26a, dated "13.V.1927.")	n.d. [1927]
4t	"Man muss unterscheiden . . ." A comment which concerns the credibility of astrology and that of astrologers. (Variant of APHORISMEN I, 26b, dated "13.V.1927.")	*1927*
4u	"Ein Opernkomponist: 'Man kann mit der Zwölf-Ton-Technik . . . nicht alles ausdrücken.'" Concerns erroneous ideas about tonality and atonality. (Variant of APHORISMEN I, 26c, dated "4.VII.1928.")	*1928*
4v	"Geheimwissenschaften sind nicht solche . . ." Concerns inborn ("angeborne") knowledge. (Variant of APHORISMEN I, 25e.)	n.d. [ca. 1928]

Dichtungen, Texte, Sprüche, Aphorismen

Designation	Subject	Description
4w	"Schönberger nennen mich manche . . ." Word play on his own name. (Variant of APHORISMEN I, 24a, dated "30/9. 1927.")	*1927*
4x	*"Meine Vorgesetzten* / Beim Militär (1916): . . ." AS names his superiors in civilian life: Beethoven, Bach, Wagner, etc. (Variant of APHORISMEN I, 24b, dated "30.9.1927.")	*1916* *[1927]*
4y	*"Nicht nur* / Ich kann mich nicht beklagen . . ." Schoenberg is pleased with his friends ("Menschen wie Adolf Loos") and also with his enemies ("W[ilhelm] Gr[oss]"). (See APHORISMEN I, 24c, dated "7.IV.1928.")	*1928*
4z	*"Wieder aus der Militärzeit:* Ein Kamerad . . ." An anecdote about an episode from AS's military service. (Variant of APHORISMEN I, 24d, dated "4.VI.1928.")	n.d. *1928*
4aa	*"Mit mir Kirschen essen* / So gefährlich es auch scheint . . ." Schoenberg makes a comment about the abuses of sayings, and mentions a poor newspaper heading, "Frisch gepflückte Lorbeeren," as another example. (See SPRACHLICHES 2 and APHORISMEN I, 17.)	*1928*
4bb	*"Der Nutzen des Falschen* / Meine Harmonielehre . . ." AS was an autodidact, but learned something from his enemies: namely, not to fear. Marginal note indicates that he planned to revise this aphorism. (Variant of APHORISMEN I, 28, dated "10.I.1924." A variant of the second part of the aphorism is found in APHORISMEN I, 25h, dated "3.VI.1928.")	*1924*
4cc	*"Schade:* / Ich hatte guten Grund[,] mich über B. zu ärgern . . ." AS makes an epigrammatic statement about anger and letterwriting. (Variant of APHORISMEN I, 24e, dated "4.VII.1928," and 49f.)	*1928*
4dd	"Dass ich Erfindungsgabe habe . . ." Concerns AS's imitators. (Variant: APHORISMEN I, 24g, dated "2.XI.29.")	*1929*

Dichtungen, Texte, Sprüche, Aphorismen

Designation	Subject	Description
4ee	"Ein Pianist, namens Diener von Schönberg . . ." AS makes a joke about another Schönberg, a concert pianist. (See APHORISMEN I, 23.)	1932
4ff	"*Meine Leidsprüche* [sic] / In der ersten, wahrscheinlich grösseren Hälfte meines Lebens . . ." Epigrammatic formulation of three stages in AS's life. (See APHORISMEN I, 16.)	1928
4gg	"*Der ehrliche Finder* / So oft ich beim Militär . . ." When in the army, Schoenberg was embarrassed to state that in civilian life his occupation was "composer." (See APHORISMEN I, 14.)	1916
4hh	"Der Komponist R. S. macht . . . Kritiker-Besuche . . ." Concerns the relationship between Schoenberg and R[ichard] S[trauss]. (See APHORISMEN I, 6a.)	1923
4ii	"Der Komponist X. sagt . . ." Comment on Richard Strauss' remark about his own themes which the most stupid fellow can understand. (See FRAGMENTE VI, 2.)	1924
4jj	"Ich springe nicht ins ganze Wasser, sondern in einen nur kleinen Teil." (Complete as is.) (See APHORISMEN I, 49g.)	1928
5.1-4	"Texte" Original and three copies of the following texts: "Unentrinnbar" and "Du sollst nicht, du musst," from the *Four Pieces for Mixed Chorus,* op. 27, together with the text for the *Three Satires,* op. 28. *A Survivor from Warsaw* is included in 3 copies (no original). *Israel Exists Again* is listed but not represented.	T.Ms., 4 p., 4to, G. & E. & Hebrew, n.p., n.d.
6.1-4	"Texte zu Kanons:" Schoenberg wrote an incomplete list of his canons, designating them by some element of the text, e.g., the dedication. Of the 11 canons listed, the texts for the following six are included in the original typescript and three copies: "für Carl Engel" (in German with an English translation), "für Dr. David Bach," "für Hugo Ganz," "für Hermann Abraham," "to Richard Rodzinski," "für Mr. Saunders." Schoenberg's plan to publish his canons	T.Ms., 2 p., 4to, G., n.p., n.d.

Aphorismen

Designation		Subject	Description
		was realized in the posthumous publication *30 Kanons,* edited by J. Rufer. Apparently Schoenberg made a slight mistake: Ganz's first name was Rudolph, not Hugo. (Another incomplete list of canons is included in KLEINE MANUSKRIPTE III, 9.)	
I *APH*	1 10	"Es besteht eine Feindschaft zwischen *Decsey* und *Kralik* . . ." Comment on music critics of the old school. Signed in ink and marked with thumbprint.	T.Ms.s., 1 p., 16mo, G., n.p. [Mödling?], *27/IV. 1923*
I *APH*	2.1 *21a*	"Grundsätze braucht nur einer . . ." Epigrammatic statement of AS's self-reliance. Signed and marked with his thumbprint.	T.Ms.s., 1 p., 16mo, G., n.p. [Mödling?] *14/III. 1923*
I *APH*	2.2 *21b*	"Grundsätze braucht nur einer . . ." Handwritten copy of above. Note at top reads: "Abschrift: *14.*VII.*32.*" With underlinings and 3 arrows AS indicates his fascination with the number correlations between the date of origin, "*14.*III.19*23*," and that of copying, "*14.*VII.*32.*"	A.Ms.s., 1 p., ink, 16mo, G., n.p. [Berlin], *14.VII.32*
I *APH*	3 22	One page with three brief aphorisms; the two earliest ones are typed, the last one is handwritten. The page is marked with AS's thumbprint.	T.Ms.s., 1 p., 8vo, G., n.p. [Mödling], *24.V.23;* with A.Ms.s., ink, G., *Traunkirchen,* *5/IX. 1923*
	3a	"Sparsamkeit: neue Schränke anfertigen lassen . . ." Ironic comment on human inertia.	
	3b	"S. Th. . . .n ist erfüllt von der Seligkeit seiner Frauen." (Complete as is.)	
	3c	"Stile herrschen, Gedanken siegen." (Complete as is.)	

Aphorismen

Designation	Subject	Description
I 4 *APH* *33*	"Ich bin nur ein *Vorläufer . . .*" Long aphorism about AS's position as a predecessor and about his imitators ("Nachläufer"). Gloss in ink referring to the word "Vorläufer," above: "So wurde ich oft in deutschen Zeitschriften genannt." Some pencil corrections. The aphorism is signed twice and marked with AS's thumbprint. (Published in Freitag, *Selbstzeugnissen,* p. 7.)	T.Ms.s., 1 p., obl. 16mo, G., *Mödling, 29.V.1923;* A.N., pencil & ink
I 5 *APH* *41*	"*Satirische Antwort /* an The Etude / An die Herausgeber . . ." Reply to questionnaire from the American music journal concerning the development of music in the next 40 years. AS states that there will be persons who believe that the highest point of development has been reached and that there will be others who lament the "decline" of the arts and praise the preceding era. Signed in ink; each page marked with AS's thumbprint. Letterhead stationary with Bernhardgasse address. Title in ink apparently added in Berlin in 1932 (see authors' introduction).	T.L.s., 2 p., 4to, pencil, G., *Mödling, 12.Juni 1923;* A.N., ink, n.p., n.d. [Berlin, 1932]
I 6 *APH* *43a-b*	Two brief aphorisms; both signed, dated (on the same day) and marked with thumbprints.	T.Ms.s., 1 p., 4to, ink, G., *Traunkirchen, 24/6. 1923*
6a *43a*	"Richard STRAUSS macht am eifrigsten Kritikerbesuche, wenn ich ein Konzert habe." (Complete as is.) (Draft for DICHTUNGEN 4hh.)	
6b *43b*	"Wenn einer davon spricht . . ." On the tendency to substitute feelings ("Gefühl") for thoughts ("Verstand").	
I 7 *APH* *63a-b*	Two aphorisms on musical issues; both signed and dated on the same day. Schoenberg used letterhead stationary with Bernhardgasse address, but crossed out the "Mödling" printed on the date line and substituted "Wien." Titles in ink apparently added in Berlin in 1932 (see authors' introduction).	A.Ms.s., 1 p., 4to, ink & pencil, G., *Wien, 29/IX. 1923;* A.N., ink, [Berlin, 1932]

Aphorismen

Designation		Subject	Description
	7a 63a	"Rich. Strauss / *R. Strauss* unterdrückt im Hofo- pernorchester . . ." Twenty years earlier Strauss conducted Mozart's G-minor Symphony with 1000 "pretty" nuances ("hübschen Nuancen"); now (1923), he does not even care for nuances, but only for money.	
	7b 63b	"Zukunftsmusik / Immer wieder wird moderne Musik geschrieben; und immer muss die Zukunftsmusik vor dieser zurücktreten." (Complete as is.)	
I	8 *MUS* 71	"Ausdrucksmusik / Da ich nie bestreiten werde, . . ." AS comments at length on Richard Strauss' obsession with self-expression. Though "Mus" is written on the item, Schoenberg classified it with the aphorisms on Ms. List A, 71: "Aph / Ausdrucksmusik / ?1923," and filed it with the aphorisms. The Ms. is signed and marked with thumbprint; the title in ink apparently was added in Berlin in 1932 (see authors' introduction).	T.Ms.s., 1 p., 8vo, G., pencil & ink, n.p. [Mödling], *1923;* A.N., ink & pencil, [Berlin, 1932]
I	9 *APH* 73	"Herr Professor / Ich habe mich lange genug gesträubt . . ." The title of Professor did not add to AS's honor. Autograph note concerns generals and doctoral titles.	T.Ms.s., 1 p., obl. 16mo, G., n.p., *20.XII.1923;* A.N.s., G., n.p., n.d.
I	10 *APH* 83	"Ist dann mein Name so genannt . . ." Schoenberg at play: is he the so-called Arnold? Note: "*Abschrift* von 82 (Denk); Aph 83."	A.Ms.s., 1 p., 8vo, G., n.p., *14.I.24*
I	11 *APH* 91	"Gespannte Unaufmerksamkeit / Er hat nur Themen geschrieben . . ." A comment on a composer (Richard Strauss) who stated that he wrote themes which the most stupid fellow can understand. (See DICHTUNGEN 4ii, and FRAGMENTE VI, 2, above.)	A.Ms.s., 1 p., 16mo, ink & pencil, G., n.p. [Mödling], *13/XIII. 1924*

Aphorismen

Designation		Subject	Description
I	12.1 *APH* *96ᵃ*	"Wie immer: wer Ochse sagt . . ." Concerns actors. Variant of 12.2, below. Autograph note on the bottom of the page reads "Rundfrage: War Wagner im Recht / in der Bühne XI 1924 / Heft 4."	T.Ms., 1 p., 8vo, carbon, G., n.p., n.d. [Mödling, 1924]; A.N., ink, G., n.p., *XI 1924*
	12.2 *APH* *96ᵇ*	"Wie immer: wer Ochse sagt . . ." Variant of 12.1, above and 13, below.	T.Ms. with A.N., 1 p., 8vo, G., n.p., n.d. [Mödling, 1924]
I	13 *APH* *97*	"Ein Schauspieler ausser Dienst . . ." Variant of above aphorisms (12.1-2), signed Jens. Quer. The item is addressed from "Thomastr. 6," Mödling (AS's Mödling address was Bernhardgasse 6). It contains the reference "'Bühne' Nr. 4, 1924, Rundfrage: War Wagner im Recht."	T.L.s., 1 p., 8vo, ink, G., *Mödling, 1924*
I	14 *APH* *101*	"Aus meinem Exerzierreglement: / Der ehrliche Finder / So oft ich beim Militär . . ." (Draft for DICHTUNGEN 4gg.)	A.Ms.s., 1 p., 16mo, pencil & ink, G., n.p., *etwa 1916*
I	15 *APH* *111ᵃ*	"*Strauss* / Mir ist . . . eingefallen . . ." The original of the item described in BIOGRAPHISCHES III, 13, above. Concerns Schoenberg's relationship to Strauss. A note indicates the copy: "Abschrift bei BIO."	A.Ms.s., 1 p., 16mo, ink, G., n.p. [Berlin] *23/V. 1926*
1	16 *APH* *121*	"*Meine Leitsprüche* / In der ersten wahrscheinlich grösseren Hälfte . . ." Written on the back of a printed thank-you letter dated "1924." (Variant of DICHTUNGEN 4ff, above.) Note at the bottom reads: "Ich wurde aufgefordert (von einer französischen Zeitung)[,] meine '*Grundsätze*' zu nennen." Refer to AS's list, "Gedruckte Artikel," no. 53: "Meine Leitsprüche (in einer Franz. Zeitschrift[)] — kein Belegexemplar / Manuskript unter APH 121."	A.Ms., 1 p., 8vo, ink, G., n.p., *1928?*

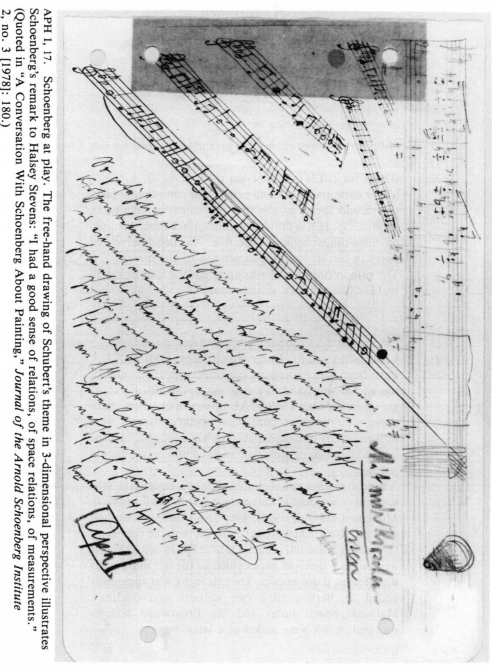

APH 1, 17. Schoenberg at play. The free-hand drawing of Schubert's theme in 3-dimensional perspective illustrates Schoenberg's remark to Halsey Stevens: "I had a good sense of relations, of space relations, of measurements." (Quoted in "A Conversation With Schoenberg About Painting," *Journal of the Arnold Schoenberg Institute* 2, no. 3 [1978]: 180.)

Aphorismen

Designation	Subject	Description

Title in crayon pencil apparently added in Berlin, 1932 (see authors' introduction).

Designation	Subject	Description
I 17 *APH* 125	*"Mit mir Kirschen essen* / So gefährlich es auch scheint . . ." (Draft for DICHTUNGEN 4aa.) Music notations in ink and pencil. The composer at play: the second theme of the first movement of Schubert's Quintet, op. 163, is drawn five times, three times distorted by third-dimensional perspective. AS also inserts tied notes to distort the time-dimension of the theme. The title in blue pencil was apparently added in Berlin in 1932 (see authors' introduction).	A.Ms., 1 p., 8vo, ink & pencil, *Roquebrune, 14/VII. 1928,* A.N., pencil, G., [Berlin, 1932]
I 18 *APH* 126	"Meine Vorbilder / Sehr geehrter Herr . . ." Letter addressed to "Robert Lyon / Revue 'MUSIQUE,'" Paris from Schoenberg in Charlottenburg. It was neither signed nor sent, and in a later note AS calls it a short article rather than a letter. AS answers a question about those who inspired him: his youthful works were influenced by popular but tasteless models; later he learned from composers who showed him how it should *not* be. A note at the bottom mentions a poor translation ("sehr schlecht übersetzt"), referring to the publication in *Musique* 1 (15 July 1928): 440. This article is found on AS's list "Gedruckte Artikel," no. 36, with the comment: "Uebersetzer ist mir unbekannt." "31" in red pencil is written on a piece of paper glued to the left margin; its significance is not known. The title in ink was apparently added in Berlin, 1932 (see authors' introduction). Marginal pencil notes and the Brentwood address stamped in ink were added at a later time.	T.L., 1 p., 4to, G., *Charlotten-burg* [Berlin], *6.VI.1928;* A.N., ink & pencil, [Berlin, 1932] and *Los Angeles* [Brentwood], n.d.
I 19 *APH* 130	"Ich halte mich für einen der schärfsten Köpfe . . ." Ironic self-evaluation.	A.Ms.s., 1 p., obl. 16mo, ink, G., n.p. [Berlin], *21.II.1928*

Aphorismen

Designation	Subject	Description

I 20.1 "Goldene Worte Mottl's / EINE SALZBURGER REDE FELIX MOTTL'S"

An extended commentary on a published lecture by a well-known musician who used Mozart to belittle contemporary composers. Schoenberg's Ms. was published in *Pult und Taktstock* (see 20.2, below). He identifies Mahler, Reger, Pfitzner, and Strauss as the targets for Mottl's speech, which was held in 1904. AS remarks that Wolf, Bruckner, and Liszt were considered too "modern" in 1904. In a marginal note he quotes from memory a poem by Mottl written against Richard Strauss. The first of the above titles was written in blue pencil, apparently in Berlin in 1932 (see authors' introduction). For unknown reasons, AS used an apostrophe with the genitive form in the later heading and inserted another one (also in blue pencil) into the original, typed heading.

T.Ms.s., with A.N., 1 p., fol., ink, G., n.p., n.d. [Mödling, 1924]; A.N., pencil & ink, [Berlin, 1932]

I 20.2
35 "EINE SEHR LEHRREICHE REDE FELIX MOTTLE"

Clipping from *Pult und Taktstock* 3 (Nov.-Dec. 1926): 159-60. The article is signed "R.K." but Schoenberg added his own signature (in ink) and wrote a note: "Stein [Erwin Stein, editor] überlassen, der es unter Jens Qu hätte veröffentlichen können, es aber K. signierte. Warum??" The number "35" stamped on the first page corresponds to AS's entry on his list "Gedruckte Artikel," no. 35: "Eine sehr lehrreiche Rede Mottl's," with the comment "unter fremder Chiffre erschienen."

P.Art.s., with A.N., 2 p., 4to, ink, n.p., n.d. [Wien, 1924]

I 21
APH
152 "Gemeinschaftsmusik . . ."

Sarcastic comment on "Gebrauchsmusik."

"Aph" is written at the bottom of the page and "153" in the top right corner. The number is apparently an error and should be "152," as Ms. List A, no. 152, reads "Aph, (Kü), Gemeinschaftsmusik, 15.3.29." No. 153 on the list is a different item entitled "Pathos."

A note reads: "Abschrift / 22.VII.32 / siehe Mus 151." The "Mus[ikalisches]" is apparently an error and should be "Kü[nstlerisches]" as Ms. List A, no. 151, reads "Kü, Musik fürs Volk, 8.7.28." The original manuscript for the aphorism is found written in ink on the verso of Kü 151. It is stamped "152," and dated "Berlin, 15/III. 1929."

A.Ms., 1 p., 8vo, ink & pencil, G., *Berlin, 15/III. 29;* A.N., n.p. [Berlin], *22.VII.32*

Aphorismen

Designation		Subject	Description
I	22 *APH* 184ᵇ	"Rationalisierung in der Musik: sie muss laufen . . ." AS is concerned with "modernen Toccaten und Concerti-grossi." Some blue pencil notes. A note reads: "Abschrift / Original bei Denk 182."	A.Ms.s., 1 p., 8vo, ink & pencil, G., n.p., [Berlin], *1930*
I	23 *APH (Witze)* 211	"Es gibt einen Diener von Schönberg . . ." (Draft for DICHTUNGEN 4ee, above.) A note at the bottom reads: "*Diener von Schönberg* heisst ein konzertierender Pianist. . . ."	A.Ms, 1 p., 8vo, ink, G., n.p. [Berlin] *23.VII.32*
I	24 *APH* 227a-g	"*Witze*[,] *Scherze* etc" Seven aphorisms collected on one 4to sheet but dated separately with the day of their conception. They were copied from older drafts, apparently in 1932 (see authors' introduction). With the exception of 24f, these drafts were later rewritten and included in the collections APHORISMEN III, 2, and DICHTUNGEN 4.	A.Ms., 2 p., 4to, ink, G., [Berlin, 1932]
	24a 227a	"*Schönberger* nennt man mich oft; . . ." (Draft for DICHTUNGEN 4w.)	[Berlin], *30/9. 1927*
	24b 227b	"Meine Vorgesetzten / Beim Militär (1916): 'In meinem Civilberuf . . .'" (Draft for DICHTUNGEN 4x.)	[Berlin], *30/9. 1927*
	24c 227c	"*Nicht nur:* Ich kann mich nicht beklagen: . . ." Concerns AS's friends (such as Adolph Loos) and enemies (such as Wilhelm Gross). (Draft for DICHTUNGEN 4y.)	[Berlin], *7.IV.1928*
	24d 227d	"*Wieder aus der Militärszeit* (1916): Ein Kamerad, . . ." (Draft for DICHTUNGEN 4z.)	[Berlin], *4.VI.1928*
	24e 227e	"*Schade!* / Wenn ich jetzt mit dem Bechert nicht bös wäre, . . ." If AS were not angry with Bechert, he would write a nasty letter to him. (Draft for DICHTUNGEN 4cc. Variant of APHORISMEN I, 49f.) A note explains that this aphorism reflects the climate of Roquebrune, where it is too pleasant for heavy thinking.	*Roquebrune, 4.VII.1928*

Aphorismen

Designation	Subject	Description
24f *227f*	*"Schritt halten!* / Ich kann mit meiner Zeit nicht mehr Schritt halten, . . ." AS composes for the future, 30-100 years ahead.	[Berlin] *16.X.1929*
24g *227g*	"Dass ich Erfindungsgabe habe, . . ." (Draft for DICHTUNGEN 4dd.)	[Berlin], *2/XI. 29*
I 25 *APH* *228*	"Aphorismen" Eleven aphorisms collected on two 8vo sheets but dated separately with the day of their conception. They were copied from older drafts, apparently in 1932 (see authors' introduction). A twelfth aphorism (25k) was added at that time. The first page is numbered "8."	A.Ms., 2 p., 8vo, ink, G., n.p. [Berlin], *23.VII.32*
25a *228a*	*"Radio* / Früher war einer, der Plattheiten verbreiten wollte . . ." Schoenberg writes a negative evaluation of the radio.	*28/V. 1927*
25b *228b*	*"Der Virtuose* / Dieser Virtuose ist ein Musiker in Taschenspiel-Format." (Complete as above.)	*28/V. 1927*
25c *228c*	*"Kleidung / Gut anziehn* / Gut anziehn muss man sich . . ." AS associates clothes and prejudices.	*12/6. 1927*
25d *228d*	*"Kontrapunkt* / Lesen, Schreiben, Rechnen . . ." Counterpoint considered as one of the basic means of developing the human mind.	*14/6. 1927*
25e *228e*	*"Geheimwissenschaften* sind nicht solche . . ." (Draft for DICHTUNGEN 4v.)	n.d.
25f *228f*	*"Leichtverständlich* / Vielen, denen meine früheren Werke gefallen haben . . ." Schoenberg maintains that his earlier works are not easier than his more recent ones.	*26/IV. 1928*
25g *228g*	*"Sechs Generationen* / Jetzt haben schon wenigstens sechs Generationen . . ." Schoenberg has survived attacks from 6 generations (of audiences).	*3.VI.1928*

*A*phorismen

Designation		Subject	Description
I	25h *228h*	"Ich bin Autodidakt . . ." (Variant of DICHTUNGEN 4bb.)	*3. VI.1928*
	25i 228i	*"Hungere! /* Raubtiere muss man . . . füttern . . ." Musicians must be starved. . . .	*6/XII.1928*
[j skipped]			
	25k *228k*	"Das Radio sendet keine tieferen Stimmen, als den Tenor . . ." AS asserts that the radio is "die Dame ohne Unterleib."	*23. VII.32*
	25 l *228l*	*"Telegraphische Zustellung /* Der preussische Unterrichts- minister . . ." AS comments on a telegraphic message from (Prof. Leo) Kestenberg to the "Gemeinschaftsmusik." Further reference is to the shortcomings of the radio: "obere Hälfte aller Musik."	*Berlin, 9.IV.1929*
I	26 *APH* *229*	"Aphorismen" Three aphorisms written on one side of a notebook sheet; another titled "Stil" on the reverse side is crossed out. Copied from older drafts and dated separately, apparently in Berlin in 1932 (see author's introduction).	A.Ms.s., 2 p., 8vo, ink, G., [Berlin , 1932]
	26a *229a*	*"Vorläufer /* Meinen ehemaligen Mitläufern . . ." (Draft for DICHTUNGEN 4s.)	*13. V.1927*
	26b *229b*	*"Astrologie /* Ich unterscheide . . ." (Draft for DICHTUNGEN 4t.)	*13. V.1927*
	26c *229c*	*"Schr.[eker] /* Man kann mit der Zwölfton Komposition . . ." (Draft for DICHTUNGEN 4u.)	*Roquebrune, 4. VII.1928*
I	27 *APH* *230*	*"Internationale Kri[e]cher /* Die internationalen Feste f. n. Musik . . ." (Draft for DICHTUNGEN 4r.) Some green pencil corrections.	A.Ms.s., 1 p., 16mo, ink & pencil, G., n.p. [Berlin], *10/II. 1926*

Aphorismen

Designation	Subject	Description
I 28 *APH* *241ᵃ*	"Der Nutzen des Falschen / Meine 'Harmonielehre' . . ." Beginning with a reference to the well-known preface to his *Harmonielehre,* AS further develops his argument that his opponents helped him by demonstrating the full consequences of wrong theories. Note at top: "Durchschlag bei Mor[alisches]." Note and title in blue pencil apparently added in Berlin in 1932 (see authors' introduction). (Draft for DICHTUNGEN 4bb.)	T.Ms.s., 2 p., 8vo, pencil, *Mödling,* *10.I.1924;* A.N., pencil, [Berlin, 1932]
I 29 *APH* *242*	Two aphorisms on small notebook page.	A.Ms.s., 1 p., 16mo, G., n.p. [Mödling]
29a	"Eben ein Feuilleton von Georg Kirchfeld [?] gelesen . . ." Comment on literary style.	pencil, *10.I.1924*
29b	"Ist der Name Arnold so genan[n]t . . ." (Variant of APHORISMEN I, 10.) A note in red pencil reads: "steht schon auf einem anderen Blatt."	ink & pencil, *11/I. 1924*
I 30 *APH* *243*	Two sets of aphorisms on two small sheets, glued back to back. On one side are drafts for the two items and on the other side are the revised, neatly-copied versions, both dated the same day.	A.Ms.s., 2 p., 16mo, ink, G., n.p. [Mödling], *6/XI. 1925*
30a	"Meine Originalität kommt daher . . ." (Draft for DICHTUNGEN 4p.)	
30b	"Meine Wünsche gehen, wenn auch spät, in Erfüllung: . . ." (Draft for DICHTUNGEN 4q.)	
I 31 *APH* *248*	"Hirn und Genie / Das Zeitalter der Romantik . . ." Short essay concerning the label once given to Mendelssohn and Schumann: "norddeutsche Verstandesmusiker." In a similar way various anti-Romantic movements after World War I neglect the unity of thought and feelings. (Variant of DICHTUNGEN 4a.)	A.Ms.s., 2 p., 16mo, ink, G., n.p. [Berlin], *4/IV. 1928*

Aphorismen

Designation	Subject	Description

<table>
<tr>
<td>

I   32
APH
257

</td>
<td>

"Ich bin nicht verdächtig[,] ein Anhänger der 'Neuen Sachlichkeit' zu sein . . ."

Schoenberg's aphorism comprises numerous marginal glosses and a lengthy note written on a newspaper article, "Hassen wir die Romantik?" by Hanns Gutman, clipped from the *Unterhaltungsblatt der Vossischen Zeitung,* no. 47, 16 February 1932. Maintaining his distance, Schoenberg opposes Gutman's argument that the ideas of "Neue Sachlichkeit" do not apply to the abstract art of music. In his opinion the application of the principles focuses on musical matters (e.g., tones, rhythms, tone-sequences) rather than on emotions or psychological phenomena.

</td>
<td>

P.Art. with A.N., 2 p., fol., ink & pencil, G., n.p. [Berlin], *16. Februar 1932*

</td>
</tr>

<tr>
<td>

I   33
APH
258

</td>
<td>

"Ich kann nicht glauben, dass Herr Wolfurt . . ."

Numerous glosses and marginal notes on a newspaper clipping of an article "Sachlichkeitsdämmerung" by Kurt von Wolfurt which appeared in the same issue as the clipping in item 32, above. Schoenberg sarcastically comments on weaknesses in Wolfurt's attack on "Neue Sachlichkeit" and in particular the author's assessment of a transitional period from about 1915 to 1935 — in the year 1932! AS writes: "schon bis 1935; also doch: Musikgeschichte auf Vorrat." (See APHORISMEN I, 36: "Musikgeschichte auf Vorrat.")

</td>
<td>

P.Art. with A.N., 1 p., fol., ink & pencil, G., n.p. [Berlin], *16. Februar 1932*

</td>
</tr>

<tr>
<td>

I   34
APH
259

</td>
<td>

"Dummes ± dumm gesagt / Dieser Wolfurt . . ."

Making a reference to a secretary at the Academy for the Arts, Kurt von Wolfurt, Schoenberg ponders the correspondance between stupid thoughts and stupid formulations.

</td>
<td>

A.Ms.s., 1 p., 16mo, ink, G., n.p. [Berlin], *31.VII.32*

</td>
</tr>

<tr>
<td>

I   35
APH
300a

</td>
<td>

"Beckmesser lässt über den Grund . . . keinen Zweifel . . ."

Schoenberg sides with Hans Sachs of *Die Meistersinger:* a shoe, like a song, must be well made, and a cobbler has the right to make songs, too.

The beginning of a second paragraph concerning Stravinsky was deleted. In a later note AS estimates that the above was written in "1921-23," but notes also that as he does not remember being concerned with *Die Meistersinger* at that time, he will file the item among the aphorisms.

</td>
<td>

A.Ms., 1 p., fol., pencil & ink, G., n.p., *1921-23;* A.N., pencil, [Berlin, 1932]

</td>
</tr>
</table>

Aphorismen

Designation		*Subject*	*Description*
		Among the notes at the bottom, apparently added in 1932, is one which refers to the carbon copy being filed in *"Verm*[ischtes]*"* (see authors' introduction).	
I	36 *APH 316*	"MUSIKGESCHICHTE AUF VORRAT / Mir schwindelte, wenn ich Jahr für Jahr . . ." A long, incomplete aphorism. Schoenberg, upset by the power and ignorance of music historians, suggests that they should write the history of music to come. The heading in blue was apparently added in Berlin in 1932 (see authors' introduction). (See APHORISMEN I, 33, above.)	A.Ms., 1 p., 8vo, ink, G., n.p., *wohl etwa 1924?;* A.N., pencil, [Berlin, 1932]
I	37 *APH 317*	"EINE MODERNE TEEKANNE / Ach ich habe eine moderne Teekanne . . ." AS laments about his modern and elegant teapot, which is totally impractical. The heading in blue pencil was apparently added in Berlin in 1932 (see authors' introduction).	A.Ms., 1 p., 16mo, ink, G., n.p., n.d.; A.N., pencil, [Berlin, 1932]
I	38 *APH 317*	"CASELLA / Herr Casella meint . . ." Casella's mistake according to Schoenberg is thinking that what is taught at conservatories is "classic" style. Heading in blue pencil was apparently added in Berlin in 1932 (see authors' introduction).	A.Ms., 1 p., 16mo, ink, G., n.p., n.d.; A.N., pencil, [Berlin, 1932]
I	39 *APH 324*	*"etwas aus mir gemacht /* Alle diese Leute haben zuerst . . ." Concerning AS's former followers, who became his enemies. A doodle and a question mark at the bottom of the page. (Draft for DICHTUNGEN 4o.)	A.Ms., 1 p., 16mo, ink & pencil, G., n.p., n.d. [ca. 1928]
I	40 *APH 325*	"Predige nicht: . . ." AS's sarcastic poem on the idea: don't try to improve things. Written on a small sheet which was glued to another 16mo sheet.	A.Ms.s., 1 p., 16mo, ink, G., n.p. [Roquebrune], *Dezember 1928*
I	41 *APH 326*	"Der Mensch ist bös! . . ." (Draft for KLEINE MANUSKRIPTE III, 2a, above.) AS added a note in ink: "Text zu einem Chor; Entwurf /	A.Ms., 1 p., 16mo, pencil, G., *Territet*

*A*phorismen

Designation		Subject	Description

		Hier sollte eine Gegen-Strophe: 'Der Mensch ist gut' folgen." He remembered writing the aphorism in *Territet oder Barcelona, 1931*. The note was apparently added in Berlin, 1932 (see authors' introduction).	*oder Barcelona;* A.N., ink, G., [Berlin, 1932]
I	42 *APH* 329	"Zu Knut Hamsuns 70. Geburtstag . . . / Man klage nicht die Zeit an! . . ." Epigrammatic birthday greeting.	A.Ms.s., 1 p., 8vo, ink, G., *Berlin, 28/VI. 1929*
I	43 *APH* 330*a-c*	"Jede blinde Henne, wenn sie nur wirklich Glück hat . . ." Incomplete essay about style and idea in music with interspersed variations on the proverb about the blind chicken that might find a grain. AS criticizes music conservatories, neoclassicism, and the current lack of understanding of Mozart's use of advanced harmonies (mentions the "Dissonance" quartet). He also specifies elements of Mozart's creative principles. A marginal note indicates "3 Blätter / 3 Seiten," which coordinates with his designation "330ᵃ⁻ᶜ" indicating 3 pages. One doodle. The item is found on the Ms. List A: 330, "1930??"	A.Ms., 3 p., fol., ink, G., n.p., n.d. [ca. 1930]
I	44 *APH* 331*a-b*	"Jeder Affe kann sowohl vierhändig, als auch zweihändig . . ." Incomplete essay on imitation (aping) in art. A small sketch in top right corner of page 1 shows six ways in which a monkey can play the piano using combinations of hands and feet. A note in the margin reads: "2 Blätter, 2 Seiten," corresponding to the "a-b" in AS's designation.	A.Ms., 2 p., 4to, pencil, G., n.p., n.d.
I	45 *APH* 332	"Jeder Esel möchte alles besser wissen, als ich . . ." A donkey was the only contemporary from whom AS learned something.	A.Ms.s., 1 p., 8vo, ink, G., n.p. [Berlin], *10/IX. 1932*
I	46 *APH* 333*a-b*	Collection of aphorisms with a recurring idea or theme. Some are complete, others are merely sketched. Note that the "a-b" in AS's designation refers to the number of pages in his Ms. Marginal notes read: "*Spinne,*" "*Hyäne,*" "Jede Krähe," "Nicht jede blinde Henne findet ein Korn," "2 Blätter."	A.Ms.s., 2 p., 4to, ink & pencil, G., n.p., n.d. [ca. 1930]

Aphorismen

Designation	Subject	Description

46a "Jeder Frosch, der eine Nachtigall singen hört . . ."
In the opinion of the unison frog chorus, the nightingale's melodic variations are "romantic" and "impractical" ("unsachlich").

46b "Jeder Vogel kann nicht einmal auf zwei Seiten zugleich sein . . ."
This aphorism, written between the lines and in the margin, is apparently a variant of 46e, below.

46c "Jede Laus liebt die Dunkelheit . . ."
Many musicians also prefer obscurity.

46d "Jeder Affe, der einen Menschen nachahmt, weiss sicherlich nicht, wer es dem Menschen vorgeafft hat."
(Complete as is.)

46e "Jeder Vogel kann nicht auf zwei Seiten zugleich sein . . ."
. . . but some musicians can. Schoenberg mentions Paul Stefan, who apparently was able to be present in two places at once, and a speculator who could not. (See KLEINE MANUSKRIPTE III, 3, and ANECDOTES 1, 2, and 3.)

46f "Jede Krähe hackt der andern kein Auge aus . . ."
This aphorism concerns musicians who lack perception.

46g "Jeder Kuckkuck"
Heading only.

46h "Jede Henne, die ein Entenei ausbrütet"
Heading only, a reference to a H. C. Andersen story.

46i "Jeder Affe denkt vierhändig"
Heading only. (See APHORISMEN I, 44.)

46j "Jeder Leithammel läuft seiner Herde nur deshalb voran . . ."
Commentary on originality.

I 47 "Manche Behauptung . . ."   A.Ms.s.,
   APH (Draft for DICHTUNGEN 4n.)   1 p., 16mo,
   343   ink, G.,
      n.p., n.d.

*A*phorismen

Designation	Subject	Description
I 48 *APH* *365*	"Wenn fünf Menschen und ein Affe . . ." Aphoristic response to article from the *Musical Courier,* dated 1 February 1936. In his column "Variations," Leonard Liebling presents a letter from Arthur Wilson of 21 January 1936, in which he relates a story about faking a piano piece in the style of Schoenberg which fools the assembled company. The aphorism is written on a card which is attached to the clipping. (See aphorism and note in DICHTUNGEN 4e.)	P.Art., 1 p., *February 1, 1936,* with attached A.Ms.s., 1 p., obl. 16mo, ink, G., n.p., n.d. [Hollywood, 1936]
I 49 *APH* *371*	Eight aphorisms written on the two sides of a sheet. Marginal glosses indicate that six of the aphorisms were copied from small notebooks which Schoenberg used during his stay in southern Europe, 1928-29. Two were added at the time of copying in Berlin, 1932.	A.Ms., 2 p., 8vo, ink, G., n.p. [Berlin], *18/IX. 1932; 7.XI.1932*
49a	"*Glück* / Man sollte nicht verächtlich . . . sprechen . . ." (Draft for DICHTENGEN 4 1, above.)	*18/IX. 1932*
49b	"*Ich als Nero* / Wenn diese drei Kritiker . . ." (Draft for DICHTUNGEN 4m, above.)	*Roquebrune, 1.V.1929;* [Berlin], *7.XI.1932*
49c	"Ich war der Meinung . . ." Schoenberg tried to improve the relationship between tones, while recent innovators merely apply a new program to old musical structures. Unfinished aphorism.	*Roquebrune, 10.I.1929*
49d	"Immer mache ich Fehler! . . ." Everybody else knows how a genius acts — only Schoenberg does not, so he is no genius. Incomplete.	*Roquebrune, 1929*
49e	"Heute Trachtenfest in Meran . . ." AS describes a parade of 52 bands, during which he constantly heard 2 or 3 groups playing simultaneously in different rhythms and keys. A "Nachtrag" reads: "folkloristisch, wie Stravinsky."	*Meran, 12.X.1930*

Aphorismen

Designation	Subject	Description

| | 49f | "Wenn ich mit dem Beckert nicht bös wäre. . ." (Draft for DICHTUNGEN 4cc. In the variant, APHORISMEN I, 24e, the name is spelled "Bechert.") | *1928.1.Juli* |

| | 49g | "Ich springe nicht ins ganze Wasser . . ." (Draft for DICHTUNGEN 4jj, above, dated 1928.) | n.d. [1928] |

| | 49h | "Gewiss wird dann erst meine Musik verstanden . . ." The arts are entangled in a marriage of convenience ("Vernunftehe"), which makes it difficult for AS's music to be understood. | *Roquebrune, 1929* |

I 50   "Warum nicht einfacher: Vom Wort als Ausdruck der Nation? . . ."

Several extensive glosses written on an off-print of a speech by Rudolf G. Binding, "Von der Kraft deutschen Worts als Ausdruck der Nation," delivered at the Prussian Art Academy in Berlin, 28 April 1933. AS is critical of Binding's use of language; he thinks [Karl] Kraus, [Berthold] Viertel or [Ludwig] Ullman have treated the subject better. Amused, he pretends to be "angenehm enttäuscht" by Binding's language (see SPRACHLICHES 2: "---angenehm enttäuscht----"). "378," "APH," and "Glossen" are written on the title page.

Description: P. Art. with A.N., 16 p., 4to, ink, G., *Berlin, 28.April 1933*

I 51   APH 382   "Meine Antwort"

This item comprises an (undated) letter from Berthold Buchenan of Munich, 7 wood-block prints by Buchenan, and a watercolor by Schoenberg. One of the prints illustrates Jacob's vision of the ladder (referring to AS's oratorio text *Die Jakobsleiter,* published in 1917), and another depicts a crucifixion scene. These two are dated 1920. The remaining four have titles which are musical terms ("Scherzo," "Allegro," "Adagio," "Finale").

In his cover letter Buchenan dedicates the wood-cut "Jakobsleiter" to Schoenberg and asks for a reply. AS's reply is the watercolor as indicated by the signature and the signed pencil note "Meine Antwort." The watercolor shows a visionary face mounted at the top of a ladder; a star is above it and a cave below. Two arrows delineate the sides; one points up, the other down. Blue figures on a black background.

Description: A.N.s., 1 p., 8vo, watercolor & pencil, G., n.p., n.d. [1920s], together with A.L. and prints signed by Buchenan, 8 p., 8vo, ink & pencil, *München, 1920*

Aphorismen

Designation	Subject	Description
51 Cover	"Gezeichnete Antwort auf eine gewidmete Zeichnung" Brown paper cover for above item. Title and "APH 382" apparently written in Brentwood in the 1940s (see authors' introduction).	A.D., 1 p., 4to, pencil, G., [Brentwood, 1940s]
I 52 *APH* *384*	"FRAGMENT: CATALAN.[ISCHES]-TENNIS / Wenn Sie wüssten, . . ." Humorous answer to a possibly-fictitious request for a comment on the state of tennis in Catalonia. Calling himself the "Musikdiktator eines Kontinents," AS states, however, that he feels himself unqualified to make an evaluation. He does comment on the fact that men and women over 30 years do not play (in Barcelona), even though tennis-players of 60, even 70, elsewhere are no longer unusual. The item possibly dates from AS's stay in Barcelona, 1931-32, but the title was apparently added in Brentwood, ca. 1940 (see authors' introduction).	T.Ms., 1 p., obl. 16mo, carbon copy, n.p., n.d. [ca. 1931]; A.N., pencil, [Brentwood, 1940s]
I 53 *APH* *385*	"Stiff Collar / A few days ago the TIMES . . . " Schoenberg makes a comment on the relative importance of composers and performers referring to a photograph that appeared in the newspaper which was taken on the occasion of a party at Otto Klemperer's home. In it Schoenberg is placed at the side, while the "big conductors" are in the center. Notes read: "unvollendet," and "copy among doublettes." The item is found on Ms. List A: 385, dated "1935."	T.Ms., 1 p., 4to, E., n.p. [Hollywood], n.d. [1935]
I 54 *APH* *386*	"Wünsche (unerfüllte)" List of prices for lessons and examinations. For example: "Interview of half an hour . . . $10 in advance." AS comments: *not* aphorism! / yet! . . ." The item is on the Ms. List A: 386, "???1934/35??"	T.Ms., 1 p., 8vo, carbon, pencil, E., n.p., n.d. [ca. 1935]
I 55 *APH* *388*	"Unintelligenz ist ja immer vielseitiger, als Intelligenz . . ." Lengthy comment attached to a clipping from the *New York Times,* 9 September 1934, "Constant Lambert's 'Music Ho'," signed by H. H., a review of Lambert's book. In his notes AS criticizes Lambert's journalistic use of indiscriminate comparisons between different art-forms and focuses on a quote from the book: "Tonality in music, as realism in painting, are a norm that is in our blood." (See DICHTUNGEN 4k.)	A.Ms., 1 p., 4to, ink, G., n.p., n.d., attached to P.Art., 1 p., fol., E., *New York, September 9, 1934*

Aphorismen

Designation	Subject	Description

<table>
<tr>
<td>I   56
APH
392</td>
<td>"Die heutige Jugend . . ."
Duplicate of aphorism in KLEINE MANUSKRIPTE II, 3, above. Signature and note in ink with tentative date: "mutmasslich vor der Abreise nach Territet; also etwa April 1931." The note was apparently added in Berlin in 1932 (see authors' introduction).</td>
<td>T.Ms., 1 p., 4to, G., n.p., April 1931; A.N.s., ink, G., [Berlin, 1932]</td>
</tr>
<tr>
<td>I   57
APH
402</td>
<td>"Man weiss heute vielleicht nicht mehr . . ."
Collection of 5 aphorisms with many deletions and corrections. Four of these are drafts for the collections APHORISMEN III, 2, and DICHTUNGEN 4, but a note on p. 2 presents a problem of dating and provenance: Schoenberg stayed in Roquebrune in 1928 and 1929, but DICHTUNGEN 4d, a variant of item 57e, was published in Anbruch already in 1926.</td>
<td>A.Ms., 2 p., 4to, ink & pencil, G., Roquebrune, n.d.; A.N.s., pencil, [Berlin, 1932]</td>
</tr>
<tr>
<td>57a</td>
<td>"Man weiss heute . . ."
(See DICHTUNGEN 4a.)</td>
<td></td>
</tr>
<tr>
<td>57b</td>
<td>"Ich habe es immer verwunderlich gefunden . . ."
(See DICHTUNGEN 4b.)</td>
<td></td>
</tr>
<tr>
<td>57c</td>
<td>"In meiner Jugend . . ."
Formerly people used the word "interesting" ("interessant") when referring to music they did not understand; now they use "practical" ("sachlich"). (Draft for DICHTUNGEN 4c.)</td>
<td></td>
</tr>
<tr>
<td>57d</td>
<td>"Aber schliesslich: warum sollte man sich bei neuer Sachlichkeit nicht wohl fühlen?"
(Complete as is.) This item was not included in the later collections.</td>
<td></td>
</tr>
<tr>
<td>57e</td>
<td>"Es heisst, die Oper . . ."
(See DICHTUNGEN 4d.)</td>
<td></td>
</tr>
<tr>
<td>I   59
APH
403</td>
<td>"MODE / So sinnlos die Mode oft scheint . . ."
Some trends in fashions, such as changing styles of vehicles, lack practical purposes; the same is true of contemporary trends in the arts. In the U.S.A., particularly in the movies and in jazz, artists compete to provide novelties and models for mass production. Fortunately, a serious composer can survive on an isolated island, trusting "die Ewigkeit des Gedankens."</td>
<td>A.Ms., with A.N., 1 p., 4to, ink & pencil, G., Roquebrune, n.d. [1929]; A.N., pencil, [Brentwood, ca. 1940]</td>
</tr>
</table>

*A*phorismen

Designation	*Subject*	*Description*

The letter "A" is written in ink at the top of the page, and in a note AS remarks that "ein Blatt B ist nicht vorhanden!" Ms. List A: no. 403, dated "1929???". Title in black crayon pencil apparently added in Brentwood, ca. 1940 (see authors' introduction).

I 59 APH 406

"PHILOSOPHY OF Mr WALLACE / Es wundert mich nicht . . ."

The item comprises an extended comment on an article clipped from an unidentified Berlin newspaper and marginal glosses written on the clipping itself. Schoenberg opposes the views of the author, Edgar Wallace, in the article "Jeder Mensch ist 'kriminell' veranlagt: Bekenntnis eines Kriminalschriftstellers," particularly with respect to the origin and relationship of laws governing social behavior. Schoenberg maintains that human beings are social by nature and that laws are formulations of their inherent dispositions.

A note, signed and dated 1 August 1932, corrects a reference in the original text from Paul Valéry to Maurice Decobra. Title in English apparently added in Brentwood, ca. 1940 (see authors' introduction).

A.Ms.s., 1 p., 4to, ink, G., n.p., *22/XII. 1928,* with A.N.s., ink, G., n.p. [Berlin], *I.VIII.32,* and A.N., pencil, E., [Brentwood, ca. 1940]; attached to P.Art., obl. 4to, [Berlin?, 1928]

I 60 APH 411

Two 16mo sheets pasted onto an 8vo sheet.

A.Ms., 1 p., 8vo, ink, G., n.p., n.d.

60a

"Das Operette / Weisheit des Theaters / Philosophie des Polytheismus / Weisheiten des Theaters sind jene . . ."

Three headings for a small note about the obvious ideas in operetta, being those that correspond to everyone's concepts, which are based on everyone's opinions and which can be projected onto stage almost without words. Doodles in the margin and a fancy frame drawn around the word, "Operette."

60b

" 'und' / Aepfel und Birne addieren / Warum man zu jeder Note ein Vorzeichen schreiben muss: . . ."

For clarity, polyphonic music needs consistent application of accidentals.

A note at the bottom states that Schoenberg will not give *Die Jakobsleiter* to U[niversal] E[dition] because they did not give him music paper on which to compose the work.

Aphorismen

Designation		Subject	Description
I	61 *APH* 423	"Wenn man mich mit diesen Ks . . . vergleicht . . ." Comparing himself with the "Ks, Schu's, Els, Hfs, Ts, Grb's etc," AS finds that he appears inoffensively unsignificant. Why then, do people not like him? A later notation identifies "Ks" as "Klemperers oder Korngold's," "T" as "Toch" and "Grb" as "Gruenberg," but puts question marks at "Schus," "Els," and "Hfs."	A.Ms.s., 1 p., 4to, ink, G., n.p. [Brentwood], *April 1939;* A.N., pencil, n.p., n.d.
II	1	"Mit Einstein 'de Strass' gebe ich mir ein Rendezvous . . ." AS expresses a wish to meet [Alfred] Einstein in 50 years in Riemann's *Musikgeschichte.* Enigmatic comment on a revised edition of Riemann's book. (See Ms. List A: no. 247, "Denk, Einstein de Strass," dated "31.II.28." The two items were possibly written at the same time.)	A.Ms., 1 p., 16mo, ink, G., n.p., n.d.
II	2	Five aphorisms on five 16mo pages, each of which is marked with a number in pencil on the lower left corner.	A.Ms., 5 p., 16mo, ink & pencil, G., n.p., n.d.
	2a 35	"Das muss schon was besonders Arges sein . . ." Aphorism with one false start crossed out in red pencil. It defines AS's use of the word "haartsträubend."	
	2b 35a	"Cultur ist das Vermögen . . ." Unfinished aphorism, followed by the revised and complete version: "Cultur ist die Fähigkeit . . ." Defines culture in terms of "Mannigfaltigkeit des Geistes."	
	2c 35b	"Sehnsucht ist das einzige positive Glück . . ." Epigrammatic expression of the opposition of longing and fulfillment.	
	2d 35c	"Wie beneide ich die jungen Leute . . ." Comment on AS's imitators. There are two versions.	
	2e 35d	"Wer niemals lügt, dem--------" (Complete as is.) This aphorism is followed by another one: "Wer immer lügt, glaubt nichteinmal, auch einem nicht[,] der stets die Wahrheit spricht." (Complete as is.) A note indicates that this was written in response to sceptical remarks about *Gurre-Lieder* made by the Viennese critic Julius Korngold.	

Aphorismen

Designation		Subject	Description
II	3	Two antithetic aphorisms about professionals vs. amateurs.	A.Ms., 1 p., 16mo, ink, G., n.p., n.d.
	3a	"I. Kunst / geht am Professionalismus zugrunde . . ."	
	3b	"II. Es ist zwar richtig, dass die Künsten . . ."	
II	4 *17*	"In der Kunst hat nicht der Klügere . . . nachzugeben . . ." Critics fail to understand that they are *behind* (meaning: secondary to) creative artists. "17" is written with pencil in the lower right corner.	A.Ms., 1 p., 16mo, pencil, G., n.p., n.d.
II	5 *25*	Two different aphorisms for an album. "25" is written in lower right corner. One doodle.	A.Ms., 1 p., 16mo, pencil & ink, G., n.p., n.d.
	5a	"Stammbuchverse für Herrn Cassirer: Pünktlichkeit ist . . ." Kings and clerks observe different rules of behavior.	
	5b	"Stammbuchverse für Herrn P.[aul] C.[assirer]: Mehr Strafe, als Racheakt." (Complete as is.)	
II	6	*"$ Don't forget that /* Vergessen wir aber nicht . . ." Schoenberg refers to the religious Indian who would die of hunger rather than butcher the sacred cows.	A.Ms., 1 p., 16mo, ink, G. & E., n.p., n.d.
II	7	"What is the difference between a secretary and his boss? . . ." Aphorism written on UCLA stationary.	A.Ms., 1 p., 4to, ink, E., *Los Angeles,* n.d. [after July 1935]
II	8	"May I state that, knowing records . . ." Schoenberg discusses different ideals for performance and comments on the notion of "perfection."	A.Ms., 3 p., 8vo, ink, E., n.p., n.d.

Aphorismen

Designation		Subject	Description
II	9	Two short comments. One concerns AS's progressing illness; the other, in interview style, comments on the prospect of atomic fall-out. Schoenberg's name and Rockingham address is typed at the bottom of the page.	T.Ms., 1 p., obl. 8vo, E., *Los Angeles* [Brentwood], *February, 1946*
	9a	"After his retirement A.S. was longtime [*sic*] very sick . . ."	
	9b	"'I am,' says A.S., 'not so much afraid of the atom bomb. . . .'"	
II	10	"We had a wire haired fox . . ." Schoenberg comments on his pet dog.	T.Ms.s., 1 p., obl. 8vo, E., *Brentwood, February 1946*
III	1	"Zu den Aphorismen kommen . . ." On the face of an envelope AS tabulated a count of pages pertaining to his planned collection of his literary texts. (See DICHTUNGEN 1, 2, 3, 5, 6.)	A.N., 1 p., 16mo, G., n.p., n.d. [1940s]
III	2.1	*"Aphorismen, Anekdoten, etc."* Autograph drafts on onion skin for the typed collection of aphorisms in DICHTUNGEN 4a-jj. Many items are dated with year of origin; the oldest, "Meine Vorgesetzten," is signed and dated "1916"; the most recent entry, "Wenn fünf Menschen . . . ," is from 1936. In 1949, Schoenberg added a note to "Abkömmlinge von meiner Musik."	A.Ms., 12 p., obl. 4to, pencil, G., n.p., n.d. [Brentwood], 1936]; A.N., 1 p., 8vo, ink, G., n.p. [Brentwood], *1949*
	2.2	Carbon copy of the Ms. in 2.1, above, lacking the added note from 1949 as described. Each page is stamped with the Brentwood address.	A.Ms., 12 p., 4to, carbon copy, G., *Los Angeles* [Brentwood], *1936*

Aphorismen

Designation		Subject	Description
	2.3	Incomplete sets of ozalid copies of 2.1.	A.Ms., 14 p., obl. 4to, copies, G., n.p., n.d.
	2 Cover	Cover made from brown paper bag. "*Aphorismen* / 12 Blätter," in pencil, and "APHORISMEN, ANEKDOTEN, ETC.," typed on the front.	A. & T.D., fol., G., [Brentwood], n.d.
IV	1	"Nur wenn die Unnatürlichkeit . . ." Collection of 9 aphorisms, incuding:	A.Ms., 2 p., fol., ink, G., Wien, n.d. [1909]

IV — 1 (continued):

> Nur wenn . . . / Die Wissenschaft . . . / Frau X . . . / Talent ist . . . / Komponierende Wunderkinder . . . / Melodie ist . . . / Kunst ist . . . / Selbstverständlich . . . / Es ist keine Schande . . .

Except for "Frau X . . ." (which concerns truth), all the above are included in the typed collection APHORISMEN VII, 1.1. Both pages are stamped on the back with the Heitzinger Hauptstrasse address.

| IV | 2 | "Kunst ist der Notschrei . . ." | T.Ms., 8 p., fol., carbon, pencil, G., n.p. [Berlin], n.d. [1909] |

IV — 2 (continued): Collection of 30 aphorisms on double sheets folded and placed inside each other. The outside sheet has no writing on the front, but the Ms. continues onto the back inside page. Page numbers and corrections in pencil. Individual aphorisms are numbered, but not in consecutive order. Several numbers are skipped and several items are unnumbered. The numbers indicate the succession of aphorisms in the printed collection as described in APHORISMEN VII, 1.1. One aphorism in this collection is not included in the published one: "Einmal ward ich sehr enttäuscht . . ."; it concerns an invention made by a young engineer friend.

| V | 1
85
C-85 | "Aphorismen / Dass der Raubmörder . . ."
Finished draft for the published collection of 14 aphorisms in APHORISMEN VII, 2. | A.Ms.s., 3 p., 4to, carbon, G., n.p., n.d. [1911] |

*A*phorismen

Designation	Subject	Description

| | 1 | "Aphorisms" | A.D., 1 p., |
| Cover | Self-made paper and cardboard folder; the above Ms. was attached with masking tape. The title is in black crayon pencil; "85" (encircled) is in green and was later changed to "C 85" with red marker. The work is presumably the same as listed in Rufer, *Works,* Writings, II.C.85. | 4to, pencil & ink, n.p., n.d. |

VI	1	"APHORISMEN / 1912"	A.Ms.s., 2 p.,
	83	Collection of aphorisms written on small (8vo, 16mo)	obl. fol.,
	C-83	pieces of paper attached with transparent tape to the	ink & pencil,
		inside of a self-made heavy paper folder. The title is	G., n.p.
		written on the cover in black crayon pencil; "83" is	[Berlin?],
		inscribed in a square at the top with black crayon pencil	*15/I. 1912*
		and later changed to "C-83" with a red marker. At the	
		head of the aphorisms "83" is inscribed in a circle; there	
		is also a note in ink: "Dem Akad. Verein geschickt." The	
		collection comprises the same six aphorisms as the printed	
		article listed in APHORISMEN VII, 3. This item is found	
		listed in Rufer, *Works,* Writings, II.C.83.	

VII	1.1	"Aphorismen von Arnold Schönberg."	P.Art., 5 p.,
	11	Printed article from *Die Musik* 9, no. 21 (1909/10):	4to, G.,
		159-63, including the following 31 aphorisms:	n.p., n.d.
			[1909]

> Kunst ist der Notschrei . . . / Talent ist die Fähigkeit . . . / Eine Sache ist des "Schweisses der Edlen Wert" . . . / Meine Neigungen . . . / Melodie ist die primitivste Ausdrucksform . . . / Komponierende Wunderkinder . . . / Das Kunstwerk ist ein Labyrinth . . . / Nur wenn die Unnatürlichkeit . . . / Wenn jemand, um was erzählen zu können . . . / Komponieren ist so leicht . . . / Der Zweck der grossen Damenhüte . . . / Mit dem ersten Gedanken . . . / Es gibt Vorgefühle . . . / Ich habe oft nicht gleich gewusst . . . / Es ist keine Schande . . . / Durch Selbstzucht . . . / Warum sind hässliche Frauen . . . / Um ihn nicht überleben zu müssen . . . / Selbstverständlich müssen Vergleiche hinken . . . / Es muss schwer sein . . . / Eine entmutigende Tatsache . . . / Der Mensch ist das, was er erlebt . . . / Wenn die Banalität . . . / Ich bin sicher . . . / Ich will ja gar nicht . . . / Wenn der Orientale . . . / Bibelübersetzung . . . / Die Wissenschaft ist eine Frau . . . / Der Kunstfreund . . . / Selbst-Ansehen . . . / Der Apostel . . .

Aphorismen

Designation		Subject	Description

Number "11" refers to AS's list "Gedruckte Artikel." "11)" is written with red pencil in top left corner. With two exceptions, "Der Mensch ist . . ." and "Wenn die Banalität . . . ," these aphorisms are all included in the typed Ms. APHORISMEN IV, 2, above. (Six of the aphorisms were published in English translation with the title "Futuristic Aphorisms" in *Etude* 41 [June 1923]: 380. Three out of the original 31 items appeared in *Melos* 18, Heft 9, 1951, p. 241, under the heading "Frühe Aphorismen." Under the same heading Reich published a selection of 17 items in *Schöpferische Konfessionen,* pp. 12-16. The entire collection is translated into Italian in Rognoni, *Espressionismo,* pp. 231-36.)

Designation		Subject	Description
	1.2	A copy of the article in 1.1, above; no marks.	P.Art., 5 p.
	1.3	A photocopy of the article in 1.1, above.	P.Art., 5 p.
	1.4	Printed galley proofs with numerous corrections in red pencil.	P.Art., 3 p., fol.
VII	2 *9* *L.9*	"Gutmann Konzert-Kalender 1911/12 / Aphorismen" Printed article which appeared in the above publication on pp. 104-06. Collection of 14 aphorisms, the same as those found in draft in KLEINE MANUSKRIPTE II, 2, described above, and also in polished form in APHORISMEN V, 1, above. The number "9" stamped on the item refers to AS's list "Gedruckte Artikel." Additional marks include "(1)," and "9)." This item is listed in Rufer, *Works,* Writings, II.L.9. (Three of the aphorisms were published in *Anbruch* 16/7 [1934]: 138.)	P.Art., 3 p., 16mo, G., n.p., n.d. [1911]
VII	3 *10*	"Aphorismen von Arnold Schönberg" Printed sheet from *Der Ruf,* February 1912, pp. 46-47. The collection contains the following:	P.Art., 1 p., 16mo, G., n.p., n.d. [1912]

Ein armer Teufel muss sich hüten . . . / Welcher Unterschied ist . . . / *Dramatische Musik:* Mir ist es verhältnismässig zu anstregend . . . / Der Kritiker könnte sich . . . begnügen . . . / Es scheint unbedingt nötig . . . / Ich liebe sie sehr . . .

*A*phorismen

Designation		*Subject*	*Description*
		The stamped "10" refers to AS's list "Gedruckte Artikel." Also, "10)" is written in red pencil. The same collection is found in the autograph Ms. APHORISMEN VI, 1.	
VII	4 *46* *37*	"Der moderne Klavierauszug" Printed article from *D ie Musik* 16, no. 2 (November 1923): 95-98. Comprises a questionnaire by M. Broesicke-Schoen with responses by 5 persons, including Schoenberg (pp. 96-97): "Arnold Schönberg, Wien: Ein Klavierauszug entsteht nicht. . . ." The single handwritten note concerns punctuation; the number "46" refers to the number of the article on AS's list, "Gedruckte Artikel." The item is stamped with the Brentwood address and annotated in blue, red, and green pencil. Reprinted in *Schriften,* pp. 191f., and in translation in *Si* 75, pp. 348-50.	P.Art. with A.N.s., 4p., 8vo, pencil, G., n.p., n.d. [November, 1923]

*A*necdotes

Designation	*Subject*	*Description*
	Three interrelated items concerning events in Austria and Germany between the wars.	
1	"This nickname derived from stories told in Vienna . . ." AS relates a series of puzzling events from the years 1912, 1919, and 1926, which in his opinion suggest that "Dr. S." [Paul Stefan] was capable of being present simultaneously at two widely separate places. Schoenberg gives credence to reports of the existence of supernatural bodies. The events involved Emil Hertzka, Rudolph Kolisch, and Dr. Marya F.[reund] ("who now lives in Mexico"). The text begins and ends abruptly, and the first line is identical to the beginning of the second paragraph of item 2, below. (See KLEINE MANUSKRIPTE III, 3, and, APHORISMEN I, 46e.)	A.Ms., 8 p., 8vo, pencil, E., n.p., n.d. [Brentwood, 1940s]

*A*necdotes

Designation		Subject	Description
	2	"Though many of the witnesses of the three stories . . ." Beginning with the second paragraph, this item is a typed revision of a portion of item 1, above. Paraphrasing a certain Viennese financier, AS gives the nickname "the bird which can be at two places at one time" to "Dr. S." [Paul Stefan].	T.Ms., 2 p., 4to, E., n.p., n.d. [Brentwood, 1940s]
	3	"He was a sweet little old man . . ." Incomplete characterization of the unidentified Viennese speculator quoted by AS in the above Mss., items 1 and 2.	A.Ms., 4 p., 4to, E., n.p., n.d. [Brentwood, 1940s]

Glossen zu den Theorien Anderer

Designation		Subject	Description
77	1	"*Hindemith, Krenek, Gutmann, Westphal . . . Wiesengrund, Redlich . . .* / Im letzten Anbruch . . ." The item comprises the first eight pages of a small purchased notebook with lined paper. The title "Glossen zu den Theorien Anderer" is written on the front together with "77" and "1929." The item is found as no. 77 on AS's Ms. List B. It was published in translation in *SI* 75, pp. 313-16.	A.Ms., 8 p., ink, G., n.p. [Berlin], *1929, Oktober 29, 15.XI.29*
77	2	"*Ueber das Volkstümliche in der Musik. / Ueber Melodie. / Ueber nationale Melodiebildung.* / Man kann nur die Gedanken ausdrücken, die man denken konnte." The item has three headings and the beginning of an essay on national characteristics in music. This was eventually crossed out. The page was stamped three times with AS's Nussbaum-Allee address; on the reverse of the sheet are some doodles. The page was tipped into the above-described notebook (see 1, above).	A.Ms., 2 p., fol., ink, G., *Charlotten-burg* [Berlin], n.d. [ca. 1929]
77	3	"Die Einheit der Elemente in der Musik." The published text from an unidentified journal ("pp. 787-88"), which is Schoenberg's answer to a question raised by Prof. Dr. Hans Mersmann in his contribution published in the same unidentified journal ("vol. 44"). A few pencil marks and one gloss are added to the text.	P.Art., with A.N., 2 p., fol., G., n.p., n.d.

Jenseitiger Querkopf

Designation	Subject	Description

The items in this category are contained in a folder and comprise Mss., tear sheets, notes with corrections, etc., related to articles written by Schoenberg's alter ego, Jenseitiger Querkopf.

1 *MUS* *88*	"Jens. Quer. / Seit die Redaktion . . ." Typed draft for second portion of article in 2, below. Signed Arnold Schönberg.	T.N.s., 1 p., 8vo, G., n.p., n.d. [Mödling, 1924]

2 *50*	"Jens Quer[s] . . ." A composite item comprising two portions of an article that appeared in *Pult und Taktstock* 1, no. 1 (1924): 8-10. The two segmnents are glued, one on each side, to an 8vo sheet on the front of which is stamped the number "50." Only a part of a note written on the face of the 8vo sheet can be read, as AS glued the first segment of the article across it; however, the item appears as no. 50 on his list "Gedruckte Artikel" with the incipit "Jens. Quers erste Aufsätze." A second note on the sheet reads "Wo ist die Polemik mit Pringsheim? / Siehe Rückseite." The first portion of the article, with the heading "Rundfrage I-III," consists of questions posed to conductors and refer to national musics, tempos, and woodwinds. A note in the margin reads "Stammen nicht auch diese von mir?" The second portion of the clipping, which begins "Seit die Redaktion . . . ," is signed "Jenseitiger Querkopf." It comprises a (ficticious) editorial commentary and three questions ("FRAGEN VON J. QU.") regarding the evaluation of conductors. (See typed draft for the second portion of this article in KLEINE MANUSKRIPTE I, 15. A handwritten draft for this portion is presently found with the literary sketches for *Die Jakobsleiter*. See Christensen, *"Jakobsleiter,"* vol. 2, p. 88.)	P.Art. with A.N., 2 p., 16mo, G. n.p., n.d. [1924] attached to A.N., 1 p., 8vo, ink & pencil, G., n.p., n.d.

3 *MUS* *94a-d*	*"Jens. Quer. über: Das Orchester der Zukunft"* Draft for the article, "Die Zukunft der Orchesterinstrumente," which appeared in *Pult und Taktstock,* vol. 1, no. 8, pp. 131ff. It is reprinted in *Schriften,* pp. 193ff., and translated into English in *SI* 75, pp. 322-26.	A.Ms.s., 4 p., fol., ink, G., n.p., [Mödling], n.d. [1924]

Jenseitiger Querkopf

Designation	Subject	Description
	AS marked the item with his thumbprint. (The typed Ms. for this article is dated "März 1924, Abschrift vollendet November 1924"; see *Schriften,* p. 492.)	
4 *MUS* 98a-[d]	"*Jens. Qu. meldet sich wieder . . .*" Draft for the article in 5, below. The "a-d" in Schoenberg's designation refers to the four pages of the item; page "d" comprises a draft for the second part of the article beginning with "Es wurde mir von der Redaktion. . . ." Signed "Jens. Quer."	T.Ms.s., 4 p., fol., ink, G., n.p. [Mödling], *December 1924, 12. December 1924*
5 *41*	"*Jens. Qu. meldet sich wieder . . .*" Printed article which appeared in *Pult und Taktstock* 1, no. 8 (December 1924): 137ff. The number "41" refers to AS's list "Gedruckte Artikel." A note reads: "*Seite 480 etc.*"	P.Art. with A.N., 3 p., 8vo, G., n.p., n.d. [Mödling, 1924]
6	"PT REDAKTION . . ." Note referring to the article in 1, above. By Jens Quer, it refers to an error in a quote.	T.N., 1 p., obl. 16mo, carbon, G., n.p. [Mödling], *31.XII.1924*

Notebooks

Designation	Subject	Description
	This category comprises a selection of Schoenberg's notebooks from the 1940s. They are similar in appearance, with oblong leaves and contain mostly miscellaneous notations in pencil and ink. Three are self-bound in black cloth, a fourth is self-bound in paper. These four contain leaves prepared with music staves. The fifth comprises loose sheets torn out of a spiral notebook.	

Notebooks

Designation	Subject	Description
I	Notebook with self-made binding, using 23 folded leaves to make a total of 48 sides. On one side of each leaf are drawn seven music staves. In this way every second page is prepared for notation of music examples. AS wrote items a - f starting from one end of the book; he then turned it over, writing items g - j starting from the other end.	A.Nb., 25 p., 16mo, ink & pencil, G. & E., *Brentwood,* n.d. [1940s]
a	A page with AS's Brentwood address and some numbers.	1 p.
b	"Avoid this mistake . . ." Clarification of the problems of passing tones. Illustrated with music example.	1 p., E.
c	Seven pages of musical examples on prepared staves.	7 p.
d	"1) coming for beauty treatment . . ." Incoherent list; includes mention of magazines for doctors' waiting rooms.	1 p., E.
e	"Exercises for the Young Composers" Suggests possible subtitles for the planned orchestration textbook. (See ORCHESTRATION, below.)	1 p., E.
f	*"Extracts of orchestral compositions"* Three non-consecutive pages (marked "A," "B," "C") of text concerning details of orchestral excerpts in particell form for use in teaching. (See ORCHESTRATION, below.)	3 p.
g	"Form in music is not for beauty." Only this sentence, the number "376," and some numerical calculations are written on the page.	1 p., E.
h	Four pages of musical examples.	4 p.
i	"The term scherzo . . ." Essay toward a definition of "scherzo" ("not a form").	3 p., E.
j	"Gesundheit ist nicht ansteckend . . ." Essay on the moral implications of suffering and on the religious/philosophic problem that good people suffer where bad ones prosper.	4 p., G.

Notebooks

Designation	Subject	Description
II	Self-made notebook bound in black cloth. It contains 19 sheets, folded along the middle to make 38 sides. Sheets are prepared so that pages with 6 ink-drawn music staves alternate with blank pages. Beginning at either end of the book, Schoenberg entered numerous comments on a variety of subjects.	A.Nb., 36 p., pencil, G., E. & F., n.p., n.d. [Brentwood, 1940s]
a	Musical notations. Unidentified sketches on 7 non-consecutive pages.	7 p.
b	"689" Miscellaneous notations: numbers and calculations (35^2, 36^2, 37^2); the note "22 / May / Presbyterian Church"; the sentence "Damit kommt man leicht hinein."	1 p., E. & G.
c	"But it would be extremely dangerous to leave the evaluation of art to the masses . . ." Commentary on the public vote on non-repertory works to be broadcast by the New York Opera. AS lists "Fidelio," "Magic Flute," "Walküre," and "Mastersingers" as examples of neglected masterpieces. He refers to Schopenhauer's concept of "auctority," and to the opposition between Handel-Bach and Brahms-Wagner.	2 p., E.
d	"The fact that almost every nation . . ." Brief commentary in which Schoenberg declares that music "tells about the mysteries of our lives, mysteries which are only accessible to the minds of faithful believers," and reiterates a belief that valuable music will survive.	3 p., E.
e	Tennis scores for opponents "Ro[nnie Schoenberg] and Bl."	2 p.
f	"REICHENBACH" List of names: "Chandler, McBride, Sumner, Bellamy, Dr. Reichenbach, Coughey, Friedlander." Also doodles.	1 p.
g	"Ce sont les pains . . ." Draft for "To the Wharfs," an article written for *SI* 50.	1 p., F.

Notebooks

Designation	Subject	Description
h	*"Tennis: love-*fifteen!" Short responses to two tennis terms "love" and "deuce."	1 p., G. & E.
i	Music sketch (3 measures), polyphonic in nature.	1 p.
j	"Monteux: 'Dissonant music is obsolete.' . . ." Comment on conservative musical trends in the U.S.A. The movement "back to Palestrina" would mean renouncing all the musical development in Europe of the last 400 years.	2 p., E.
k	"Ronnie / Petersen" Tennis scores for son Ronald and his opponent Petersen. Written on 5 non-consecutive pages.	5 p.
l	"Why do Boxers, football players [and] tennis players not weare [*sic*] black tie-suits when they are faced by the spectators. (Complete as is. See DICHTUNGEN 4j, above.)	1 p., E.
m	Short musical notation of a row and inversion. The row is from *A Survivor from Warsaw.* It is notated in the bass clef.	1 p.
n	"Leichtentritt in einem höchst servilen Artikel . . ." Schoenberg is critical of Leichtentritt's characterization of the principle of inversion as "aesthetic." AS prefers to compare it to geometric figures.	1 p., G. & E.
o	Telephone number.	1 p.
p	"Division = Hauptteil" A list of musical terms in English with German equivalents.	1 p., G. & E.
q	Musical notation. An example of imitation and a descending chromatic scale.	1 p.
r	"Hotel 40 . . ." A financial accounting, including tips.	1 p., E.

Notebooks

Designation		Subject	Description
	s	"Das ist ein Selbst Porträt / gefällt es dir nicht / XIXI selbst." The entry comprises only this text and a drawing. (See facsimile in C. Steuermann, "Schoenberg at Play," *JASI* 2, no. 3 [June 1978]: 247.)	1 p., G.
	t	*"ham, tongue . . ."* List of conserved food items and clothes, apparently to be shipped to Europe. A note reads, "unsolicited gift / once a month."	1 p., E.
	u	"Arnold Schoenberg" Handwriting exercises. AS wrote his name forwards, backwards, upside-down, and with both right and left hands.	1 p.
III		A notebook in a self-made paper binding. Six music staves drawn in ink on each alternating page. Contents comprise incomplete short drafts or sketches for essays on musical topics and musical examples. Schoenberg began his writing from both ends of the book.	A.Nb., 32 p., 16mo, ink & pencil, E. & G., n.p., n.d. [Brentwood, 1940s]
	a	"Unless the Allmighty plants a genius . . ." Essay on the relationship between national resources and music. Mentions Czechs, Hungarians, Dutch, Finns, Poles, and "folk-music."	3 p., E.
	b	"richest cadence in classics: Eroica . . ." Note on harmonic "regions," harmonic features in Beethoven and Liszt, with some musical examples.	1 p., E.
	c	"My subject: Beauty and Logic in music . . ." Essay in which Schoenberg expresses his view that beauty is a by-product of the exploration of musical ideas; "musical logic" is the consequent implication of such ideas. He considers the tension between the overtones of two or more tones as a generating force in music comparable to the sexual tension between man and woman, which he explains [with a quote from his own *Modern Psalms* (Psalm 10)] as the expression of the energy of life still unborn.	5 p., E & G.

Notebooks

Designation	Subject	Description
IV	A notebook with a self-made cloth binding and 32 pages, only 6 of which have writing. Schoenberg's Brentwood address is stamped inside the cover. The contents comprise a draft for an essay and some musical notations.	A.Nb., 7 p., obl. 16mo, ink & pencil, E., *Los Angeles* [Brentwood], *June 20, 47*
a	"In Haydn and Mozart still some of the principles of odd construction . . ." Like Beethoven, these two composers had a "longing" for the use of contrapuntal combinations. Harmonic simplicity was no limitation in Beethoven's case: he was a "great Rhythmiker and Tondichter." Schubert's harmonic richness was balanced as he "kept his phrases within certain limits." Some musical examples.	6 p., E. & G.
V	The item comprises 22 loose leaves (44 p.) from a purchased spiral-bound notebook. Thirty-one pages contain writing. The Brentwood address is stamped on one page.	A.Ms., 31 p., obl. 16mo, ink & pencil, E., *Los Angeles* [Brentwood], 1940s
a	"The emotional side . . ." Brief statement concerning the elements of music that determine moods: contrasting modes, tempi, and dynamics.	1 p.
b	"I have no reason of [*sic*] being idle [vain?] . . ." Draft for an article about caricatures. At the top is a frame inside which is written "photo," and in the body of the text is an empty frame meant to contain a caricature. AS compares the technique of caricatures to those of musical variations and refers to Beethoven, op. 133, and Wagner. Some musical examples.	14 p., ink

Notebooks

Designation	Subject	Description
c	"Which is the influence of war on composition? . . ." Draft for essay in which Schoenberg mentions Socrates, Nietzsche, Heinrich Schütz, Beethoven, and Napoleon. One musical example.	16p., pencil

Orchestration

Designation		Subject	Description
		Collection of materials relating to Schoenberg's planned textbook for orchestration. The contents comprise drafts for the text, lists of teaching materials, a collection of musical examples, and drafts for letters, among other things. Rufer, *Works,* p. 139, describes some of the materials. None of the items in Schoenberg's earlier orchestration project of 1917 is found here. (See NOTEBOOKS I, e & f, above.)	
I	1.1	"*CLASSICAL SCORE EXTRACTS* / for the Use of Beginners in Orchestration" Draft for text, with the original title "Materials for Orchestration" crossed out.	T.Ms., 15 p., 4to, E., n.p., n.d. [Brentwood, late 1940s]
	1.2	"*MATERIALS FOR ORCHESTRATION*" Copy of the draft above, 1.1, with some corrections and additions.	T.Ms., 16 p., 4to, carbon, E., n.p., n.d. [Brentwood, late 1940s]
	1.3	"*CLASSICAL SCORE EXTRACTS* / for the Use of Beginners in Orchestration" Ozalid copy of pages 1-2 of the draft for the text with corrections.	T.Ms., 2 p., 4to, ozalid copy, E., n.p., n.d. [Brentwood, late 1940s]

Orchestration

Designation		Subject	Description
I	2	Notations of corrections and additions to the above draft.	A.N., 2 p., 4to, pencil, E., n.p., n.d. [Brentwood, late 1940s]
I	3	"1. omit . . . / 2. whose 2 hands are co-ordinated . . ." Suggested corrections to the text above coordinated by number. Written by Leonard Stein.	A.N., 1 p., 4to, pencil, E., n.p., n.d.
I	4.1	"Extracts of orchestral compositions . . ." Suggested corrections for above draft.	T.Ms., 2 p., 4to, E., n.p., n.d. [Brentwood, late 1940s]
	4.2	"Extracts of orchestral compositions . . ." Carbon copy of 4.1, above.	
I	5.1	"There is also perhaps the possibility. . ." The copyright notation on this document, "copyright by Arnold Schoenberg 1949," is the composer's confirmation of the dates appearing elsewhere (see 8 and 9, below).	T.Ms.s., 1 p., 4to, E., n.p. [Brentwood], *1949*
	5.2-3	Two carbon copies of 5.1, above.	
I	6.1	"Orchestration / It might be useful for the teacher as well as for the student . . ."	T.Ms., 2 p., 4to, E., n.p., n.d. [Brentwood, late 1940s]

Orchestration

Designation		*Subject*	*Description*
	6.2-3	Two carbon copies of 6.1, above.	
I	7	"MATERIALS FOR ORCHESTRATION" Single-spaced copy of the text in 1.1-3, above, with details of organization indicated.	T.Ms., 12 p., 8vo, E., n.p., n.d. [Brentwood, late 1940s]
I	8.1	"Mr. Arnold Schoenberg has contrived a method of extracting . . ." Draft for an announcement of Schoenberg's method for teaching orchestration with a description of the teaching implements required: books with extracts for the students, and recordings with master-scores for the teachers. The last paragraph raises the question of copyright.	T.L., 1 p., 4to, E., n.p. [Brentwood], *January 3, 1949*
	8.2	Carbon copy of 8.1, above.	
I	9	"Mr. Schoenberg has contrived a method of teaching . . ." Form letter to be sent to select American composers requesting extracts of works for Schoenberg's use in his text. It is apparently written by AS's assistant Richard Hoffmann. AS's Brentwood address is found at the top, Hoffmann's west Los Angeles address is found typed at the bottom, together with Hoffmann's name. He requests that the composer select 5 or more examples of 8-16 measures of different character.	T.L., 1 p., 4to, E., *Los Angeles* [Brentwood], *June 1, 1949*
I	10	"Rules of Producing Parts of My Orchestral Works" Schoenberg's conditions for allowing reproduction of his own scores.	T.Ms. with A.N., 1 p., 4to, E., n.p. [Brentwood], *October, 1945*

Orchestration

Designation		Subject	Description
II	1	Orchestration examples. With some duplicates, separated from each other.	A.N., 1 p., obl. 16mo, pencil, E., n.p., n.d. [Brentwood, late 1940s]
II	2	A small purchased spiral-bound notebook, which comprises 11 pages of writing.	A.Nb., 11 p., 16mo, pencil, E., n.p., n.d., [Brentwood, late 1940s]
	2a	"nature gave instinct . . ." Outline for essay on nature, religion, law, war, and on the aims of education and culture.	5 p.
	2b	An accounting of expenditures ("Car, 6.50 . . . ," etc).	1 p.
	2c	"pre Bach (bass[o] continuo) 5[%] . . ." List of some 27 composers from whose works Schoenberg planned to take excerpts for his orchestration text; Brahms is not included. AS indicated the percentage of space he wished to devote to each. He anticipated "about 400 ex. on 100 pages.	2 p.
	2d	"20 / 25 - 5. - . . ." Figures having something to do with the monetary value of quarters.	1 p.
	2e	"Vera Laserson" Name and Los Angeles address of the above named person.	1 p.
	2f	"Ruth Pallock" Name and Manhattan Beach address of the above named person.	1 p.

Orchestration

Designation		Subject	Description
II	3.1	List of 21 excerpts.	T.Ms., 1 p., 8vo, E., n.p., n.d. [Brentwood, late 1940s]
	3.2	Carbon copy of 3.1, above.	
II	4	Unidentified excerpts copied from sources.	A.Ms., 5 p., 4to, pencil, n.p., n.d. [Brentwood, late 1940s]
II	5	*"Strings alone"* List of excerpts from Beethoven's Symphonies 1 and 2: "Strings alone" (p. 1) and "Wood alone" (p. 2).	A.N., 2 p., 16mo, pencil, n.p., n.d. [Brentwood, late 1940s]
II	6	"Before I transcribed some Bach organ music . . ." The beginning of an essay on the importance of the study of complex contrapuntal textures before beginning the study of orchestration.	A.Ms., 1 p., 8vo, E., n.p., n.d. [Brentwood, late 1940s]
II	7	Outline and notes for an orchestration text.	A.Ms., 9 p., 8vo, pencil, E., n.p., n.d. [Brentwood, late 1940s]

Orchestration

Designation		*Subject*	*Description*

7a   *"Combinations"*   7 p.

Schoenberg's outline for his text is found on seven numbered ("I-VII") pages. Headings include:

> *"Combinations,"* a list of all possible groupings of orchestral instruments in sections and varied groups with divisi and soli combinations;
>
> *"FORMS,"* including symphonic, concerto forms, dance music, orchestra with basso continuo, and opera;
>
> *"Character, mood, illustration,"* a list ranging from "gay, vivace . . ." to "soft, dreamy . . . ," including "horse riding (Valkyrie), hammering (Siegfried) . . .";
>
> *"Stiles* [*sic*] (technical)," a list of musical textures from homophonic to contrapuntal;
>
> " . . . times," a list of musical styles from "pre-classical" to "new";
>
> *"Composers,"* a list of some 70 composers' names by nationality and in chronological order. Note that Brahms' name does not appear on the list, which includes such others as Halévy, Walton, Gershwin, and Chopin, the latter with two question marks.

On p. VII, Schoenberg notes that "the examples are <u>graded</u>" and are presented in order of difficulty.

7b   "Abbreviations"   2 p.

Alphabetized list of abbreviations for use in the text.

II   8   Music notations comprising some examples for the orchestration text.   A.Ms., 1 p., 4to, and 8 p., 8vo, ozalid copies, n.p., n.d. [Brentwood, late 1940s]

Orchestration

Designation	Subject	Description
III	Self-bound notebook with 26 pages. The last 16 pages are not used.	A.Nb., 10 p., obl. 16mo, ink, E., n.p., n.d. [Brentwood, late 1940s]
a	"If you wanted to write a piece for piano . . ." Schoenberg draws a parallel between the composer of orchestral music working at the piano and the sculptor sketching in clay, or the architect designing on paper. The piano is a means, and the student who is taught to write at the piano scores mechanically and misses the point. Marginal glosses mention instances of surprising instrumentation in Mozart's *Jupiter Symphony*.	10 p.

Miscellaneous

Designation	Subject	Description
1	Doodles on the letter "B," and the following notation: A - D D - B A - D G - C - G - B - D	A.N., 2 p., obl. 16mo, pencil, n.p., n.d.
2	"Theme a 1-10 . . ." Two sheets on which As tested his device for drawing staves. One page contains a list of measure numbers for the theme, variations, and coda of an unidentified piece.	A.N., 2 p., 8vo, pen & ink, E., n.p., n.d.
3	Notation of a row and its inversion. Doodles.	A.N., 1 p., 8vo, pencil, n.p., n.d.

Appendix I

List of Categories

Aesthetik

      a) Musik Theorie

          auch theoret[ische]   Polemik u[nd] $\boxed{\text{Mus}}$

               ''   Glossen

      b) Alle andern Künste

          auch Glossen u[nd] Polemik

          auch zu eigenen Schriften und Malereien $\boxed{\text{Kü}}$

Meine   Theorien

             Deutungen

             Erklärungen

             Erfindungen $\boxed{\text{Deut}}$

             Vorschläge

             Verbesserungen

Denkmäler

      Porträts (auch sympath[ische])

      Erlebnisse ⎫

                ⎬ u[nd] Personen   Denk

      Abenteuer ⎭

      Pranger

Vermischte Gedanken

      auch Politisches

             Wirtschaftliches   Verm

             Soziales

List of Categories

Natur, Physik, Tiere   Nat

Sprachliches auch Glossen   Spr

Aphorismen, Scherze, Witze[,] Satiren
       Glossen, Polemik
       ohne theoretische Bedeutung   *Aph*

Anekdoten
       Erlebnisse etc   An

Moral
       Lebensanschauung
       Weltanschauung
       Philosophisches   *Mor*
       Lebensweisheit

Biographisches
       auch über Entstehung
          der Werke   *Bio*

Appendix II

List of Manuscripts [Ms. List A]

1	Mus	Kunst Golem	15/VII 22
2a	Mus		??1913-1914
b	(Abschrift)	Musikhistoriker	
3	Verm	Sem[inar] f[ür] Kom[position]	1/9 1917
4	Mus	Wiederholung	1913-14?
5a		Nachpfeifen	1913-14?
b	Abschrift unvollendet		
6a	Mus	Ostinato	13/V.1922
b	(Abschrift)		
7	Mus	Fundament	25/III 23
8	Spr.	Schupo	7.IV.23
9	Nat	Nachtigall	10.IV.23
10	Aph	Decsey – Kralik	27/IV.23
11	Spr.	November-Verbrecher	26/IV.23
12	Spr	Schlusspunkte	10.IV.23
13	Denk	Klein Zaches (ich bedaure es sehr!)	29.V.23
14	Mus	Polytonalisten	21/IV.23
15	Denk	Wiener-Kärntner	27/IV.23
16	Denk	St. Stefan	18.IV.23
17	Verm	Verwandtschaft	16.IV.23
18	Mus	Hauer[,] Gesetze	8.V.23
19	Mus	'' Kosmische Gesetze	9.V.23

List of Manuscripts [Ms. List A]

20	Mus.	Komp[osition] m[it] 12 Tö[nen]	9.V.23
21a	Aph.	Grundsätze	14.III.23
b		Abschrift	
22	Aph.	Sparsamkeit, S. Th..	24.V.23
		Stile	5.IX.23
23	Mus	Quellenvergifter Riemann	18.V.23
24	Mus	Transposition	12.V.23
25	Deut	Habsburger	22.V.23
26	*Bio*	Meine Schrift	28.V.23
27a	Mus	Dr Unger: Tonbewusstein	
b			3.III.23
c	drei Blätter, 3 Seiten Text		
28	Mus	Gelehrsamkeit	25/V.23
29	Deut	Bourgeoisierung d[er] Pol[itik]	28.V.23
30	Spr.	Neuland der Paletten	24.V.23
31a	Mus	Stricharten u[nd] Sevcik	30.V.23
b		2 Blätter	
32	Denk	Brief an Fr. W.	28.V.23
33	Aph	Vorläufer	29.V.23
34	Mus	Symmetrie	11.VI.23
35	Mor	W[r] Konzerthausgesellsch[aft]	24.V.23
36	Mus	Schenker [-] Polemik	Juni 23
37	Mus	Schenker ″	6.VI.23
38	Spr.	Ludendorf	8.VI.23
39	Verm	Untergangs-Raunzer	9.VI.23
40	Mus	Polyphonie-Leute	11.VI.23
41	Aph	Satir[ische] Antw[ort] an The Etude	12.VI.23
42	Mus	Zur Notenschrift	26.VI.23
43	Aph	a) Strauss	24.VI.23
		b) Gefühl u[nd] Verstand	
44	Verm	Israeliten und Juden	5.VII.23
45a	Mus	Meine Bezeichnungstech[nik]	6.VII.23
b	″	Wiederholung	″
46a	Mus	Zeitungsausschnitt	
b		Missverst[ändniss] d[es] Kontrap[unkts]	6.VII.23
47	Mus	Bogen	7.VII.23

List of Manuscripts [Ms. List A]

48	Denk	Rösch	17.VII.23
49	Mus	Theoretiker[-]Hirn	9.VII.23
50	*Bio*	Ruhe	20/VII.32
51	Mus	Vortragszeichen	16.VII.32
52	Deut	Belagerte Festung	20/VII.23
53	Mus	Verzierungen u[nd] Konstruktion	20/VII.23
54a b	Mus	Stichverbesserung	28/VII.23
55a b c d	Mus }	Zeitungsausschn[itt] H. Riemanns Betonungsschema; mit Glossen Kritik: Zur *Metrik*	} 10.VIII.23
56	Mus	Zur Darstellung des Gedankens	19.VIII.23
57	Mus	Parallelengesetz	20.VIII.23
58a b c	Mus	3 Blätter: *Die Jugend und ich* und 2 Nachträge hierzu 58 d e	25/IX.1923 wohl viel früher
59	Mus	Imitatoren (Kuhlau)	24.VIII.23
60	Bio	Meine Nichtberufung	24.VIII.23
61	Mus	Geschichtsparallelen	5/IX.23
62	Verm	Der Gegenspieler	26/IX.23
63a b	Aph	Rich. Strauss Zukunftsmusik	) 29/IX.23) ein Blatt
64	Mus.	Die Absäger an der Arbeit	29/IX.23
65a b c	Mus	Neue Musik 3 Blätter, 3 Seiten	29.IX.23
66a b c	Mus	Zur Terminologie der Formenlehre 3 Blätter = 3 Seiten	5/X.23
67a b c	Mus	Hauers Theorien	9/XI 23 bio?[?]
68	Denk	Rich. Strauss als Agitator	Novbr 23
69	Mus	Polytonalisten	29.XI.23
ˣ70a b c d	Mus	Ich und die Zeitgenossen (4 Blätter 4 Seiten)	5.XII.23

List of Manuscripts [Ms. List A]

71	Aph	Ausdrucksmusik	? 1923
72	Mus	Notenbilderschrift	10.XI.23
73	Aph	Herr Professor	20/XII.23
74	Bio	Sühne	5/XI.23
75	Mus	Sprung über d[en] Schatten 2 Seiten	21.XII.23
76	Mus	Kunstgeheimnisse	22/XII.23
77	Mor	Der Geldjude	Ende 23 ?
78a b	Mus Spr	Fuga-Flucht	10/1.24
79	Bio	Requiem	15/XI.23
80	Mor.	Theoretiker	10/I.24
81	Verm	Wiederabdruck der Richtlinien	Januar 1924
82a b	Denk Bio	Hofrat Triebenbacher	15.I.24
83	Aph	Arnold genan[n]t	11.1.24
84	Bio	Lebensgeschichte in Begegnungen	15.I.24
85abcdef A B	Mus Kü	6 kleine Blätter Formenlehre	29.I.24
86a b	Mus	Studierpartitur	1.II.24
87	Denk	Eine Abrechnung	2.2. 24
88	Mus	Jens Quer	1924
89	Bio	Nochmals Sühne	17.II.24
90	Mus	Vorwort zu Weberns kleinen Quartettstücken	Juni 1924
91	Aph	Gespannte Unaufmerksamkeit	13/III.24
92	Bio	50 *ter*	20.VIII.24
93abcd	Mor	Beilagen Stellung zum Zionismus	12.3.24
94abcd 4 Seiten/	*Mus* Abschrift	Jens Quer über: *Das Orchester der Zukunft*	1924? oder 23?
95	Bio	Inschrift für Trude	1924
96ab	Aph	War Wagner im Recht?	XI.1924

List of Manuscripts [Ms. List A]

97	Aph	Ein Schaupieler ausser Dienst Jens Quer	XI.1924
98a b c d	*Mus*	Jens Qu meldet sich wieder-- Pringsheim	XII.24
99	Mus	Berichtigung hierzu	31.XII.24
100 a b	Mus } Bio }	Polytonales bei mir	12/XII 24
101	Aph	Der ehrliche Finder	1916?
102	Mor	Brief an einen Pianisten	10/VIII.1925
103	Spr	Wasserlandung	14.VIII.25
104	Mus	Zu „Darstell[ung] d[es] Gedankens" 2 Blätter, 3 Seiten	21/XI.25
105	Mus	Herr Bruno Weigl	5/X.25
106	Mus	Johann Strauss	25/X.25
107	Mus	Amerikanische Rundfrage über Jazz wo gedruckt[?]	? 1925
108	Bio	*Blicke*	1./6.26
109	Mus	Wert der Harmonielehre	10/II.26
110	Deut	Schreibmaschine	25 oder 1926
111a	Aph	Rich[.] Strauss	23/V.1926
b	Bio	dasselbe[,] Abschrift	21.VII.32
112	Mus	Kleiber dirigiert Bruckner	11.4.26
113	Denk	Kreneks „gehaltener Vortrag"	etwa 1926?
114	Mus	*Klemperer*	7.III.28
115a b	Bio	Zeitungsausschnitt Karpath über Bösendorfer	X.28
116	Deut	Messer in den Mund	3.II.28
117	Deut	Pumpernickel siehe [225]	? 1928
118	Denk	Brief an 8ʰ Abendblatt	30.V.28
119	Denk	Florizels Geister	13.VIII.28
120	Verm	Conzert Gebouw[-]Feier	1928?
121	Aph	Meine Leitsprüche	1928?
122	Verm	Ver[einigung] d[er] Aut[oren] d[er] U[niversal] E[dition] Auffford[erung]	1928?

List of Manuscripts [Ms. List A]

123	Verm	Fragebogen üb[er] Ver[einigung] d[er] Aut[oren] d[er] U]niversal] E[dition]		1928?
124	Bio	Endlich allein		4.II.28
125	Aph	Mit mir Kirschen essen		14.VII.28
126	Aph	Meine Vorbilder		6.VI.28
127	Kü	Gemeinschaftskunst		28.2.28
128	Denk	Der Mediokre		18.7.28
129a b	Kü	Inspiration	2 Blätter 3 Seiten	1926?
130	Aph	Denkfehler		21/II 1928
131a b c	Mus	Stravinskys Oedipus ein Blatt		24/II.28
132	Deut	Unruhen in Wien		24./8.28
133	Denk	Herr Muck		12/II.28
134	Bio	Glocken am Thury		vollendet 20.VII.32
135	Bio	Das Tempo der Entwicklung		?1928
136	Mus	Zukunft der Oper		24/XII.27
137	Mus	Zur Metronomisierung		25/X.26
138	''	''		1926
139	''	''		8.XI.26
140	''	Versuch über Dissonanzen		?
141	Deut	Schreibmaschine		?
142	Spr	Die kernige Elsa		Mai 27
143	Mus	Meine Sackgasse		23.VII.26
144	Mus	Der Restaurateur		24.8.27
145	Mus	Gutachten ü[ber] e[ine] neue Notenschrift Notenschrift (Akad[emie])		[n.d.]
146	Mus	Křenek für leichte Musik		25/2.26
147	Denk	Gratulation an Bach		28/7 24
148	Denk	Julia Culp	u[nd]	28.V.28 20.VII.32
149	Bio a b c d	Beantwortung wissenschaftlicher Fragen (4 Blätter, 4 Seiten und Durchschlag [)]		etwa 1928

List of Manuscripts [Ms. List A]

150	Aph	Goldene Worte Mottls	ohne Datum
151	Kü	Musik fürs Volk	8.7.28
152	Aph (Kü)	Gemeinschaftsmusik	15.3.29
153	Kü	Pathos	8.4.28
154	Mus	Oktavenklänge u[nd] Gänge [?]	17/XII.25
155	Verm	Grundlagen ästh[etischer] Bewertung (ein Anfang)	offenbar vor der Pariser Reise
156	Verm	Musik fürs Volk	15.6.28
157	"	Fortsetzung	16.6.28
158a b	*Verm*	Die Lehrer	25/8 28
159	Mus	Die alten Formen in der neuen Musik	10.7.28
160	Mus	Musikalische Dynamik	5.4.29
161	Bio	Schaffensqual Original unter Mus	7.4.28
162	Kü ⎫ 	Anti Kritik-Lob des Verstandes	29.9.27
163	Kü ⎬ ein Blatt	Herz und Hirn	29.9.27
164	Kü ⎭	Tiefe	30.9.27
165	Mus	Disposition eines Lehrbuchs des Kontrapunkts	24.11.29
166	Mus	Die Urform der Cambiata	⎰ April ⎱ 1932
167	Kü	Theater-Reise 1931	22.12.31
168	Mor	Entwicklung—Fortschritt	19.1.32
169	Mus	Phrasierung	7/2.31
170	*Mus*	Der lineare Kontrapunkt 5 Blätter, 9 Seiten	2.12.31
171	*Mus* 4 Blätter, 7 Seiten	Instrumentation	23/XI.31
172	Mus	Der Kritiker Rob. Schumann a) Zeitungsausschnitt b, c, d, 3 kleine Blättschen	11.11.31
173	*Mus* a b c	*Raumton, Vibrato, Radio* etc 3 Blätter, 5 Seiten	5.1.31

List of Manuscripts [Ms. List A]

174a b	*Mus*	Konstruktives in der Verkl[ärten] Nacht	Februar 1932
175	*Mus*	Notierung — Vorzeichen	18.1.31
176	*Mor*	Liebe deinen Nächsten	19.7.26
177	Mor a *Mus* b	Durchführung	19.7.26?
178	Verm	Mein Stil	31.1.31
179	Denk	Ueber Franz Schreker	III od[er] IV.31
180	Kü	Schönheitsgefühle	4.IX.31
181 a-g	Kü	Stuckenschmidt[,] Brecht: Operngesetze, 7 Blätter, 7 Seiten	3.VIII.31
182	Denk	Schreker (Flexaton)	9.5.29
183a b	Denk	Klemperer (Abschrift und Original)	3.V.30
184a b	Denk Aph	Rationalisierung der Music . . . Abschrift	} 1930?
185	Denk	Trude	8.I.29
186a b	Denk	Couvert u[nd] Brief an Frau Dubost[,] Paris	9.X.28
187a b	Denk 1 Blatt	Der Allgem[eine] Deut[sche] Musikverein Nachtrag	24/V.28 6.XII.28
188a b	Denk	D$^{\underline{r}}$ Graf, Monn-Bearbeitungen 2 Blätter, 3 Seiten	11.5.28
189	''	auf der 4. Seite[:] H. H. *Stuckenschmidt* und	6.4.29
190^a_b	''	*Wallaschek* u[nd] *Bienenfeld*	8.4.29
190$\underline{b}$	Denk	Stilblüten lügnerischer Feinde b) Nachtrag hierzu	} 23.VII.32
191a	Mus ein Zettel 191b zu Denk	Respighi — Selberaner Mit Nachtrag von 7.4.28	26.9.27
192		Deutsch	28.9.27
193	Denk 1 Blatt 2 Seiten	Eisler	8.7.28
194		nochmals Eisler	13.7.28

List of Manuscripts [Ms. List A]

195	Mus	Aus einem Gutachten für die Akademie	14.12.29
196	Mus	Die italienische Nationalmusik 2 Blätter, 2 Seiten	25.9.27
197	Mus	Kammermusik	ohne Datierung
198	Denk	Herr Petschnig 3 Blätter, 6 Seiten	7.7.27
199	Denk a b, c,	Zeitungsausschnitt Florizels Geister 2 Blätter, 3 Seiten	16.12.31
200 } 201 }	Denk ein Blatt	De Falla Busoni (Prater = Italien)	1.XII.31 23.7.32
202	Pranger	Herr v. Milenkovic	25.11.31
203a b	Denk	Was man nicht vergessen sollte (2 Blätter, 3 Seiten)	2.12.31
204	Denk a b c d e	Die Universal Edition resp. – Herr Herzka kleine Notizen sehr unvollständig	5.VII.27 13.V.28
205	Mus	Nachtrag z[um] Vorwort der Satiren 1 Blatt, 2 Seiten	26.9.27
206	Mus	Zu Werkers Bach-Studien	20.9.28
207	Mor	Schopenhauer u[nd] Sokrates	23.7.27
208	Kü	Zu „Der biblische Weg"	5/VII.27
209	Spr	Stilblüten	3.8.27
210a b	Kü	ein Blatt zu „Sprich zu dem Felsen" (Der bibl[ische] Weg)	12.VI.27 23.VI.27
211	Aph	Diener von Schönberg	23.VII.32
212 213	Mus } ein Blatt }	Alter und neuer Kontrapunkt Händel über Gluck	10.VI.28 6.12.28
214	Mus	Bach u[nd] d[ie] 12 Töne	23.VII.32
215a b c d	Spr	Aberhundert Das ist nicht gesagt „Derselbe" Sprache der Reklame	29.V.27 23.VI.27 3.VII.27 5.9.27

List of Manuscripts [Ms. List A]

e		Qualitätsware	5.9.27
f		7 billige Handschuhtage	''
g		Die Deutschesten	25.V.28
h		Tennis-Sprache	25.V.28
i		Karpath	3.4.29
k		Der substanzarme Eigenbrötler	6.4.29
216a	Deut	Ein alter (trauriger[?]) Hase	27.5.27
216b	3	Weineinschenken	27.5.27
216c	Blätter,		
216d	sechs	Hühneraugen	28.5.27
	Seiten	Habtacht	28.5.27
216e		Sprache der Tiere	28.5.27
216f		Kravatte u[nd] Pulswärmer	28.5.27
216g		Gernhaben	28.5.27
216h		Vormerkung anderer Redensarten	[n.d.]
217	Deut) 1	Kleidung	12.6.27
	} Blatt		
218	Deut)	Bügelfalte	1.12.27
219	Deut)	Krankheiten	
	{	Sodbrennen	13.6.27
220	Deut)	Grippe Rezidiven	Nachträge
		2 Blätter, 4 Seiten	Oktober 30
			Juli 32
221)	Deut	Tiere: Hunde	23.VI.27
222 {		Hunde	30.XI.27
	1 Blatt		
223 /	2 Seiten	Hunde	13.X.27
224 \	Deut	Habtacht (Nachtrag [)]	23.VI.27
225 {	ein	Pumpernickel	15.X.27
	Blatt	siehe 117	
	2 Seiten		
226 /		Ethnologisches	8.VII.28
227a	Aph	Schönberger	30.IX.27
b		Meine Vorgesetzten	30.IX.27
c	Scherze	Nicht nur	7.IV.28
d	Witze	Meine Handschuhe	4.6.28
e		Schade	4.VII.28
f		Schritt halten!	16.X.29
g		Meine Erfindungsgabe	2.11.29
228	Aph	a) Radio	28.5.27
ein	''	b) Der Virtuose	28.5.27
Blatt	''	c) Gut anziehen	12.6.27
	''	d) Kontrapunkt	14.6.27

For rows 227a–g the bracketed annotation reads: 1 Blatt 2 Seiten

List of Manuscripts [Ms. List A]

zwei	Aph	e) Geheimwissenschaften	14.6.27
Seiten	''	f) Leichtverständlich	26.4.28
	''	g) Sechs Generationen	3.6.28
	''	h) Ich bin Autodidakt	3.6.28
	''	i) Hungere	6.12.28
	''	k) Dame ohne Unterleib	23.7.32
	''	l) Telegraphische Zustellung	9.4.29
229	Aph	a) Vorläufer u[nd] Mitläufer	13.5.27
ein	''	b) Astrologie	13.V.27
Blatt	''	c) Schreker	7.VII.28
1	Denk	d) dasselbe[,] Abschrift	27.VII.32
Seite			
230	Aph	Internationale Kriecher	10.2.26
231	Mor	Glaubwürdigkeit der Wahrheit	29.II.32
232	Verm	Nationaler Aufmarschplan	anfangs 1932
233	Verm	Die Elektrische und der Autobus	19.I.30 od[er] 31
234	Denk	Neid	22.X.28
235	Denk	Herm. Wolffs Bruder	13.5.28
236	Denk } ein Blatt	Herr Lendvai	13.5.28
237a	''	Skandal b[ei] d[en] Variationen op. 31	16.10.29
b	Bio	Abschrift 23.7.32	23.7.32
c	An	Zettel -	'' '' ''
238	Na	Mathematik	23/IV.27
239	Verm	Vortrag: Schutzfrist u[nd] Verlängerung 3 Blätter, 4 Seiten	26.IV.27 27.IV.27
240	Verm a b	Vorschl[ag]:Intern[ationale] Stilbildungsschule 2 Blätter, 2 Seiten	März 1927
241a	APH	Der Nutzen des Falschen	} 10.I.24
b	Mor	Durchschlag	
242	Aph	2 Aphorismen siehe 83	{ 10.I.24 { 11.I.24
243	Aph	Meine Originalität } mit einer Abschrift Meine Wünsche }	6.11.25
244a	Deut	Stahl-Schärfe	20.12.25
b		2 Blätter, 3 Seiten	
245	Deut	Temperatur u[nd] Puls 1 Blatt, 2 Seiten	20.12.25

List of Manuscripts [Ms. List A]

246	*Denk*	Glückl[iche] Hand in Breslau	27.III.28
247	*Denk*	Einstein de Strass	31.III.28
248	*Aph*	Hirn u[nd] Genie	4.IV.28
249	*Denk*	Der Abseher	18.IV.28
250	*Verm*	Professionalismus	IV.28
251	*Mus*	Linearer Kontrapunkt Lineare Polyphonie	? 28??
ohne Nr. Bio		Verzeichnis der gedruckten Aufsätze etc	[n.d.]
252	Denk	Bondy Nachtrag, Rückseite	17.IX.1930 31.VII.32
253	Verm	Ueber die Kritik	15.11.30
254	Verm a-e	Wirtschaftliches	2.11.30
255 in einem Heft	*Mus*	Glossen zu Redlich, D[ie] kompositorische Situation v[on] 1930[.] Anbruch VI.30	Juni 1930
256	*Mus*	*Krenek:* Fortschritt u[nd] *Reaktion* 8 Blätter Glossen angefügt im Heft d[es] Anbruchs	''
257	Aph	*Glossen:* „Hassen wir die Romantik? " v[on] Hans Gutmann	Voss[ische] Zeit[ung] v[on] 16.II.32
258	Aph	Glossen zu: *Sachlichkeitsdämmerung* v[on] Wolfurt	''
259	Aph	*Dieser Wolfurt* Dummes ± dumm gesagt	31.VII.32
260	Deut 2	Nahe Berge	2.V.32
261	'' Blätter	Beleuchtete Finsternis	''
262	'' 4 Seiten	Beim Augenarzt	'' und 16.VII.32
263	*Verm*	Entwicklung	[n.d]
264	*Verm*	Soziales-Wirtschaftliches 5 Blätter, 10 Seiten	26.XI.31
265	*Verm*	Ueber: Spanisches Tennis	Mai 32
266	*Denk*	Paul Stefan, der Biograph	1932?
267	*Denk*	Versuch eines Nachrufs für Herzka	Mai 1932

List of Manuscripts [Ms. List A]

268	*Verm*	Entwurf eines Aufsatzes *Notenvervielfältigung* 7 Blätter	März 1932
269	Verm	Merkmale der Logik	II.32
		ein Blatt	
270	''	Partitur u[nd] Stimmenherstellung	29.II.32
271	*Denk*	Noch zu errichtende Denkmäler	32
272	*Verm*	Entw[urf] [eines] satir[ischen] Aufsatz[es] Psycho-Analyse u[nd] Musik	1932
273	*Mus*	a) *Notenschrift und Spiegel-Canons* b) Der Violinschlüssel	21.VI.31 16.11.31
274	*Mus*	ein unvollendeter Aufsatz „*Nationale Musik* ["] 11 Blätter, 1-7 u[nd] a-d	Februar oder März 1931
275	*Mus*	Zu: *Darstellung des musikalischen* *Gedankens* 2 Blätter, 2 Seiten	16.VIII.31
276	*Mus*	Entw[urf] z[um] Vorwort d[er] Komp[ositions] Lehre	17.VIII.31
277	*Mus*	Waltershausen 6 Blätter, 6 Seiten	11.VI.31
278	Kü	Soll der Komponist v[om] Kritiker lernen?	März 31
279	Denk	Strobel Uebersteigerter Individualismus	31
280	*Mus*	Ueber eine neue Notenschrift Gutachten (Akademie)	? etwa 1927?
281	*Bio*	Briefentwurf a[n] d[ie] Int[ernationale] Ges[ellschaft] f[ür] neue Musik	etwa 1926
282	*Verm*	Strassenbahn-Fahrschein	Januar 1927
283	*Verm*	Gegen die Räuberpflage	1922 oder 23 ?
284	*Kü*	Begrüssung des sprechenden Films	Februar 1927
285	*Bio*	Brief an die U[niversal] E[dition]	1923
286	*Verm*	Aufnahmebedingungen	1926
287	*Mus*	Auffassungs-Schwierigkeiten	?
288	*Mus*	Rundfrage: Einfluss des Jazz (Entwurf)	?

List of Manuscripts [Ms. List A]

289	*Bio*	Todes-Vision Willettes (siehe Jakobsleiter[)]	1926
290a b	*Mus*	Die (Rund =) Frage[,] wie man zu Beethoven steht	1927
291a b	*Mus*	Tonalität	a) 1923 oder 24 b) 3.VIII.1932
292	*Kü*	Schutzfrist (Akademie[)] mit Glossen	?
293	*Deut*	Tarchinieren[?] veränderte Abschrift	b ? a 3.VIII.32
294	*Mor*	Gut und schlecht	?
295	*Bio* siehe 306	*Interview mit A.S.* von Jens Qu[er]	siehe 306 1925?
296	*Bio*	Berichtigung	?
297a) b)	*Mus* *Kü*	Zu "Darstellung des Gedankens„ Abschrift	3.VIII.1932
298a) b)	*Mus* *Dubl*	Entwurf: Vortrag[,] Gesellsch[aft] f[ür] Akustik u[nd] Phonetik Durchschlag	Oktober 26
299	*Mus* *Kü*	Zur „Vortragslehre["] Durchschlag	a ? b
300	*Aph* *Verm*	a Schuhe und Gedichte b (Durchschlag)	?
301	*Denk* *Pranger*	Biograf N? 2	2. u[nd] 3. I.26
302	*Mus*	Entwicklung der Harmonie	?
303	*Verm* *Mor*	a Hohe u[nd] Niedere b (Abschrift)	? 3.VIII.32
304	*Kü*	*Kunst u[nd] Revolution*	??1919 oder 20
305	*Mus*	Regers Violinkonzert	etwa 1923
306	*Bio* siehe 295	Jens Qu[er]: interviewet A.Sch.	siehe 295 13.III.25
307	*Denk*	Herr Prof. Lach	[n.d.]
308	*Mus*	Rhythmik	30/VI.25
309	*Mus*	Stravinsky über seine Musik mit Glossen von August 1932	[n.d.]
310	*Mus*	zur Vortragslehre	1923?

List of Manuscripts [Ms. List A]

311	*Verm*	Die allgem[eine] Musik[-]Volksschule	??1911?
312	*Mus*	Die Zukunft der Orgel	??1906/7??
313	Kü	Falscher Alarm (Pfitzner)	etwa 1910?
314	Kü	Aufsatz über Loos	17/I.1926
315	Mus	Volksmusik u[nd] Kunstmusik	vor 1926
316	Aph	Musikgesch[ichte] auf Vorrat	?
317	ʺ	Eine moderne Teekanne	?
318	ʺ	Casella	?
319	*Bio*	Antwort an Zemlinsky auf eine böshafte Frage	17.VI.25
320	*Kü*	Kriterien des Wertes des musikalischen Kunstwerkes	?
321	*Kü*	Theater der Dichtung	1931
322	Spr.	Der ehrlich zugebende Dieb	?
323	*Verm*	Aufstellungsschema für die Gurrelieder	1917 oder 18
324	*Aph*	Etwas aus mir gemacht	?
325	Aph	Predige nicht	Dezember 1928
326	*Aph*	Der Mensch ist bös	1931
327a b c	*Verm*	Abonnenten neuer Musik	1918/19
328	*Kü*	Viel oder wenig probieren	23.II.31
329	Aph	Zu Knut Hamsuns 70[.]-Geb[urtstag]	28.VI.29
330a b c	*Aph*	Jede blinde Henne	1930/?? 31
331a b	ʺ	Jeder Affe	?
332	ʺ	Jeder Esel	10.9.32
333a b	ʺ	Jeder Frosch, Jede Laus, Jeder Affe, Jeder Vogel, Jede Krähe, Jeder Leithammel	30 oder 31 ʺ
334	*Bio*	Puccini über mich	1930?
335	Mus Ausschrift bei Dubletten	Zur Formenlehre	ohne Datum

List of Manuscripts [Ms. List A]

336	*Kü*		Rücksicht auf das Publikum	[n.d.]
337	*Kü*		'' ''	?
338	*Verm*	2 Blätter	Tennis (Aufschlag und Zu[illegible])	1928
339 a, b	*Mus*		Bachbearbeitung an Stiedry	31.VIII.30
340	*Mus* *Kü*		Brief an Ibach Abschrift bei Kü	[n.d.]
341	*Verm*		Der Gedanke u[nd] die Zange [?]	
342	*Verm*		Der neue Musikunterricht	24.III.29
343	*Aph*		Manche Behauptung	?
344	*Deut*		O Mensch	21.XII.28
345	*Denk*		Nationale Dichtung	8.IX.32
346	*Denk*		Herr Urban (B[erliner] Z[eitung])	28 oder 29
347	*Denk*		Ich und die Hegemonie in der Musik	XII.28
348	*Denk*		Elsa	1928
349	''		Elsa	1928
350*	Bio		Malerische Einflüsse	1938

351**	Die Entstehung der Musik	Mus	9,6,1932
352	The concept of form	Mus	1938
353	Toscanini	Denk	7,18,37
354	Stefan George	Denk	10,12,32
355	Meine Gegner	Bio	X,5 32
356	Diebe Ia: Herzka a) b)	Bio	after 1924
357	Glaserer, Rassismus, Kleine Hunde	Verm	1933
358a,b	Männer und Worte	Verm	1933
359	Spengler: Moral ist Schwäche	Mor	X,10,32
360	Kulturführer	Mor	X,13, 32
361	. . . an meinem Überfluss	Bio	XI,12,32

---

* This is the last entry of the handwritten portion of the list. At the bottom of the page is the following handwritten note: "Zahlreiche Gutachten für die Akademie der Künste."

** Here begins the typed portion of the list. Each page carries the following headings indicating the contents of the four columns: "No," "Title," "Folder," and "Date," respectively.

List of Manuscripts [Ms. List A]

362	Grüssen	Deut	XII,27,33
363	Wirtschaftliches	Deut	X.6.32
364	Das Neugeborene	Deut	IX,8,1932
365	Wenn fünf Menschen und ein Affe	Aph	????1933/4
366	Neue Wörter: Geburtlichkeit und Verfestigung	Sprach	IX.5.32
367	Loyalste Zollrevision	Sprach	IX,28,32
368	Wo ist ein gestohlener Revolver geblieben? Sofortprogramm	Sprach	32 oder 33?
369	Arbeit für mich	Spr	X.8.32
370	. . angenehm enttäuscht . . keine Lorbe(e)r(e)n [sic] gepflückt "Gehobene" Stände	Spr	Ende 32
371	Glück (1932), Ich als Nero (1929) Verbesserung der Verh[ältnisse] zw[ischen] Tönen[,] Ich mache Fehler, -Trachtenfest (1928)[,] Vernunftehe	Aph	
372	Rangesfragen	Bio	1932 u[nd] 33
373	Symphonische Form	Mus	about 38
374	Die Fuge ist . . .	Mus	8.8.36
375	6-7-8- & 9-stimmige Akkorde mit Leittonschritt-Aufl[ösung]	Mus	36-38?
376	Mahlers 25. Todestag	Mus	IX.8.1932*
377	Weltwirtschaft a) Brief an xxxxx? b) Vorschlag zur Lösung	DEUT	Herbst 1933
378	Von der Kraft Deutschen Wortes als Ausdruck der Nation	*Aph* (Glossen)	1933
379	Mahler-Bund, Brief an Mengelberg enthaltend "Demokratie"	BIO	1921 oder 22
380	Walter Pieau—Freund meiner Jugend	Bio	vielleicht 26??
381	Vorwort zu Steins Führer	Bio	?????
382	Gezeichnete Antwort	APH	????????
383	Notizen zu Klavier[-]Auszug	Mus	zwischen 16 und 18

---

* 1932 is erroneous. Mahler died in 1911, and the correct year should have been 1936.

List of Manuscripts [Ms. List A]

384	Fragment: Catalanisches Tennis	APH	1932
385	Stiff collar	APH	1935
386	Wünsche	APH	???1934/35???
387	Reputation?	BIO	1935
388	Vielseitige Unintelligenz (Constant Lambert)	APH	[n.d.]
389	Hitlers Kulturbolschewisten	Mor	Probably 1933
390	Die photographische Intelligenz des grössten lebenden Musikers	MUS	1935
391	Ankündigung von Kursen	BIO	1934 or 35
392	Die heutige Jugend.	APH	??1931??
393	Mein Gesuch um Zulassung als Privatdozent	BIO	30.8.32
394	Zwei sehr wichtige Definitionen a) RHYTHMUS b) CONTRAPUNKT	MUS	27.VIII.32
395	Macht, Mehrheit, Faschismus	DEUT	20.VIII.32
396	Max Liebermann und die Tradition	BIO	20. u[nd] 27.8.32
397	Politik (Wie ich die Habsburger retten wollte[)]	DEUT	10.IX.32
398	Krolls unsinnige Vorrede	MUS	24.VIII.32
399	Staat	DEUT	20/VIII/32
400	Die Priorität	BIO	10/11/IX,32
401	Notizen zu Kunstwert und Rückseite: LOOS	MUS	ohne Datum
402	Norddeutsche Verstandesmusik[,] Falsch intonierte Dreiklänge[,] . . . interessant . . . Blatt II: Opernkrise	APH	1929???
403	Mode	APH	1929???
404	Technische Probleme und Gemeinschaftskunst	MUS	1929
405	Aufführungserlebnisse	BIO	ohne Datum 1929?
406	The philosophy of Mr. Wallace	APH	12/XII,32
407	Berg über meinen "Berliner" Konzertskandal	BIO	4.12.28

List of Manuscripts [Ms. List A]

408	Glossen zu "Krach '*um*' (autour de) Schönberg ["]	BIO	1928
409	Krenek über Schubert	MUS	1928
410	Der Musiker Weill	Mus	27/XII.1928
411	Weisheiten des Theaters	APH	?????
412	Notes: Preface to Suite	MUS	??1934/5?
413	Amerika und Japan	Deut	XII/28 37
414	Entwürfe (Zeichnungen) Glieder[ung] d[es] Judth.[,] Schreibmasch[ine] etc	Verm	. . . .
415	Fragments: [a)] Teaching, b) Kontrapunkt im 19. u[nd] 20. Jhdt	MUS	??
416	Es gibt kein Entrinnen copies, English under Manuskripte, Doubletten und Raritäten	BIO	May 4, 1940
417	Nicht mehr ein Deutscher	BIO	about 1928?
418	(Geplantes) Rundschreiben: Beschwerde wegen Ablehnung durch AKM*	BIO	about 1935 or 6
419	A) Without a permanent Visa	*BIO*	1935
	B) Letter to a good Businessman		
420	A) Letter to Mr. Olin Downes about Suite f. Str. Orch. — not mailed	*MUS*	1935
	B) Criticisms by Downes and Gilman		*''*
421	Analysis by ear (A) B/C[:] 2 small sketches	MUS	?1935?
422	Why do we make it so difficult to our children	VERM	1939?
423	Meine sympathische Unbedeutendheit	APH	1939
424	Genie — eine Entwicklungsstufe	DEUT	17/XI.35
425	Vorwort zum Programm der Erstaufführung des ersten Teils der Gurrelieder, Skizze und Reinschrift, Copy under Doubletten	BIO	1908
426	Analyse des I. Streichquartetts für die Tonkünstlerfest Auff[ührung]	*MUS*	1905 or 6
427**	WEBERN	DENK	1940

---

* Österreichische Gesellschaft der Autoren, Komponisten und Musikverleger.

** The last entry is handwritten in ink.

Appendix III

List of Manuscripts of Articles, Essays, Sketches, etc. [Ms. List B]

1	Die Zukunft der Orgel (2)	1904 ???
2	Warum neue Melodien (1)	1913
3	Gewissheit (2)	1919
4	Briefanfang (an Anbruch) (1)	?? 1920 ??
5	Brief an UE, unabgeschicht (4)	1923
6	50er Geburtstag (1)	1924
7	Glosse (Ueber das Gute . . .) (1/2)	?????
8	Aufnahme in die Meisterklassen	1925 ??
9	Tonalitaet und Gliederung (4) (maschin)	1925
10	'' '' '' '' '' '' (4) (Handschr)	1925
11	Gesinnung oder Erkenntnis (8 1/2)	
12a/b	Der Sprechende Film (handschr) (2)	1927
13	'' '' '' (maschin) (1)	''
14	Notizen z.[u einem] freien Vortrag (1)	? 27 ?
15	Jeder Ochse (handschr) (3)	1929
16	Mein Publikum (1) Sketches	1930
17	'' '' (5) (Masch)	1930
18	a&b Entwuerfe zu Loos' 60tem Geb.[urts] T.[ag] c. Brief an den Bürgermeister	1930 1930
19	Artikel f.[ür] die Loos-Festschrift	1930
20	Zur Kompositionslehre, handschr. (11)	1930?
21	Zur Formenlehre. Durchschr. von Kleine Ms (2)	??

List of Manuscripts of Articles, Essays, Sketches, etc. [Ms. List B]

22	Speeches on the Records of the four Stringquartets (7)	December 1936
37*	On George Gershwin's Funeral (1)	1937
38	George Gershwin (4)	1937
39a	Letter to L. Liebling (not mailed) (2)	1937
b	paper page (1)	
40	Fuer ein Alban Berg-Buch, 40a (7)	1936???
	40b—Explanation why not printed	1940
41	Fragment: "Teaching without a method"	1939
42	Preface to the records of the Str. Qu. (7)	1937
43	Teaching and modern trends in music	1938??
44	About the Kol Nidre	1938
45	The Technic of the Opera Composer a free lecture	1939
46	Rundschreiben zum 60. [Geburtstag] (2) (an Freunde)	1934
47	Rundschreiben: Bericht an Fernerstehende (3)	1934
48	Glosse: Dirigenten (one, 1)	1934
49	A four Point Program for Jewry (37)	1938
50	Art and the Moving Pictures (7)	1940
51	Wien, Wien, nur Du allein (2 & a cart)	1939
52**	Zu Mahlers 50. Todestag (Fragment und Briefe) (4)	1936
53	a), b) letters to Mrs. McCormick (not sent off) 2 sheets informations c) about Greissle d) about Görgi (4)	1938
54	Notizen zum Brahms-Vortrag, Frankfurt (18 slips)	1933
55	Notes to How can . . [a music student earn a living] and Eartr.[aining] through . . [composing] etc	1938
56	Notes and drafts to Met.[hod] of Comp[osing] w[ith] 12 tones	1934
57	Manuscr / Success and Value (9)	1935
58	Manuscr: When we young Austrian Jewish [Artists] (4)	1935
59	Fragment of a speech (in German) to be spoken at a reception in New York (5)	1933
60	Notes on Kol Nidre and 4 point Program (8)	1938
61	Fragment on my music (2)	???

---

* The list is non-consecutive: nos. 23-36 are found following no. 79. AS marked this by placing a sign in the margin between nos. 22 and 37.

**See note to Ms. List A, no. 376, p. 127.

List of Manuscripts of Articles, Essays, Sketches, etc. [Ms. List B]

62	2 fragments on Jewish affairs (15)	perhaps about 1937?
63	Fragment on Organization of Mus. Dep. UCLA	1937
64	Entwurf der Statuten des Mahlerbundes	1921
65	Entwürfe zu Moses und Aron-1926 (3)	1926
66	Entwürfe zu einem Drama	1928
67	Kriegs-Wolkentagebuch	1914
68	Tagebuch	1912
69	Entwürfe zu S e r a p h i t a	???? 1918
70	Die Musik der Parteifreunde und andere Fragm[ente]	???? 1908
71	Meine Music [. . .] und Ueber die Oper	vor 1930
72	Druckvorschriften für E r w a r t u n g	1914
73	Meine Notenschreibmaschine, Patentschrift, Beschreibung, Zeichnung etc	1909
74	Neue Musik (Meine, s.[iehe] a.[uch] 71) (14)	??1928?
75	Busoni's Aesthetik, mit Glossen	??1909
76	Kriterien musikalischen Wertes, Entwurf.	1927
77	Glossen zu Theorien	1929
78	Fahrkarte für die Strassenbahn	?1928???
79	Ankündigung (Kurse) & Briefentwürfe	??1934??
	Between No 22 and 37 all the numbers were omitted. These numbers will here be used now	
23	Studien zu Kol Nidre	1938
24	Entwurf zu Richtlinien für ein Kunstamt	1919
25	Beiträge (Artrud's) zu einem geplanten ABBRUCH	1925??
26	Zeichnungen, Tramwaykarte, Letterchecks . . .	??1924/1940
27	Stichanweisungen & Gl.[ückliche] H[and], Wien 1924	
28	Vorwort und Texte zu op. 27 & 28	1925/26
29	Kleine Manuskripte I ⎫	
30	" " " II ⎬ Inhalt siehe spezielle ⎭ Listen *	
31	Meine Kriegspsychose und die der anderen	1914
32	Manuskript[,] M A H L E R - Vortrag	1912
33	Notizen zu Probleme der Harmonie	1927

---

* See tables of content at the end of the list.

List of Manuscripts of Articles, Essays, Sketches, etc. [Ms. List B]

34	Notizen zu Vortrag "Variationen f.[ür] Orchester.["] Frankfurt	
35	Kleine Manuskripte (Das Wiener Str. Qu. etc.)	
36	Notizen, freier Vortrag "Schutzfrist"	
80	2 fragments: a) for an opera	1909????
	b) 1st steps to Jakobsleiter	1910????
81	Abbreviations UCLA	1938
82	Ideas, Notes, Sketches, Fragments	
83	Aphorisms	15/I 1912
84	For (a) and Against Karl Kraus (b)	
85	Aphorisms	
86	Entwurf einer Polemik	
87	Das Verhältnis zum Text	??? 1912
88	Sachgemäss	
89	Liszt	
90	Plan einer Musikzeitung	
91*	There is no escape	July 29 1940
92	Seven Fragments A-G, no dates, but probably before 1900	
93/94		
	93: Aphorismen, published 1910 or 11 in "Die Musik"	
	a) Bleistift-Original	1910 or 11
	b) Maschin-Kopie	
	94: Internationale militärische Friedenssicherung	
	a) 1ste Niederschrift, Bleistift	1917
	b) Durchschlag der Reinschrift, ebenfalls Bleistift	
95	Originalhandschrift: "Probleme des Kunstunterrichts"	1911??
96	Encouraging the lesser master: a contribution to a book edited by José Rodriguez who also helped me correct my errors and copied the final version: 96A.	
	96B is my original	1940
97	Notes to the preceeding (Enc. the lesser master)	
98-101	Vorworte, Druckvorschriften, Texte und andere	
102-107	Bestandteile von op. 27 und 28 und der "T E X T E"	

---

* No. 91 is written in ink, possibly by Gertrud Schoenberg.

List of Manuscripts of Articles, Essays, Sketches, etc. [Ms. List B]

98	Vorwort zu Texte (unbenützt) (1. Fassung)
99	″ ″ ″ , 2. Fassung
100	Vorwort zu op. 27 und 28 (unbenützt)
101	Manuskripte A Der neue Klassizismus B Du sollst nicht, du musst C Vielseitigkeit, Am Scheideweg, Unentrinnbar
102	Notes to Preface to Opus 27 and 28
103	Manuscripts of some of the texts to op 27/28 (5 sheets-handwritten, partly)
104	A) Vorwort, 1st version B) ″ 2nd ″ , hand., p. 1, 2, 3 C) Various notes D) ″ ″ and Druckanweisungen E) Notes to the Vorwort F) Druckanweisung
105	A - D Stich- u.[nd] Druckanweisungen und "Vorbemerkungen["] zu op 27/28
106	(unbenütztes) Vorwort zu op 27/28, Reinschrift, Masch
107	″ ″ zu op 27/28, Handschrift
108	Ein Notizbuch mit Ideen (auch musikalischen)
109	Wer mit der Welt Laufen will Text eines Geburtstagskanons für Dr. D. J. Bach
110	Unterrichtsbedingungen (niemals akzeptierte)
111	Meine Zeitgenossen, ein Artikel, wahrscheinlich für eine Amerikanische Zeitschrift: kein Belegexemplar!
112	Akademie der Künste zu Berlin Beethoven Kuratorium (etc?)
113	Entwürfe zu Moses und Aron
114*	Folkloristic Symphonies, English
115	Symphonien aus Volkslieder, my translation, in German
116	Is it fair?
117	On revient toujours. 1948

---

* Nos. 114-39 are in Richard Hoffmann's, Arnold Schoenberg's (and possibly Gertrud Schoenberg's) handwriting.

List of Manuscripts of Articles, Essays, Sketches, etc. [Ms. List B]

118   Blessing, Today's Manner, Blessing (ok),
            Maturity (Self-analysis), OK

119   Thanks to the National Institute of Arts and Letters

120   Criteria for the Evaluation of Music

121   My Evolution   (also German translation, "Rückblick")

122   Menschenrechte

123

1. To Become Recognized	2. Alban Berg
3. Ehrenbürger	4. Letter to Fassett
5. My Attitude towards Politics	6. The Task of the Teacher

124   *a* The Story of the Third Trombone   *b* For the Radio Broadcast of the String Trio May 1949

            c In answer to Koussevitzky's article "Justice to Composers"   *d* Tennis Symbols

            e Letter of Thanks in reply to 75th birthday congratulations

125   *a* Bach I, II, III, IV;   *b* Cadenza;   *c* Politics
            d Preface to the Columbia recording of "Pierrot Lunaire"

126   *a* Analysis of the Kammer- symphonie   *b* For My Broadcast
            c Pumpernickel   *d* My Way
            e Three Pieces for Piano   (?)*f* Some letters: to the Regents of the University of California, to Stokowsky, to Jelivets [Jalowetz]

127   Napoléon Patience   (German)

128   Program Notes

129   Cadenza (1951?),* "Gurrelieder" (1951), "Klangfarbenmelodien" (1951)

130   1) Every Strike . . . (1951)   2) Peace Treaties.   (1951)
            3) Körpertemperatur (1950)

131   Dankbrief für die Ernennung zum Ehren Presidenten [*sic*]
            der Israel Academy of Music

132   *a* Der kleine Muck,   *b* If I were today . . .
            c Uraufführung meiner Variationen
            d When for 8 Months I lived in Barcelona . . .

133   Wiesengrund

134   Moderne Psalmen

---

* The dates at nos. 129 and 130 are later additions.

List of Manuscripts of Articles, Essays, Sketches, etc. [Ms. List B]

135   Beginning of a lecture to have been broadcast by the BBC.

136   *a* Copyright Law ⎫
                        unfinished
     b Subordination ⎭
     c A few lines about the tragic death of Rolf Hoffmann

137   Notes & remarks

138   Sketches for a cloverleaf underpass for a highway

139   ⎰ *a* Israel Exists again   *b* ?Hymn (deutsch) 1949
     ⎱ Microfilmed & in envelope with other sketches: Chorwerke 418a etc.
          c Aphorism? "Tiefe? . . ."

Addenda to Manuscript List B*

[1]
Vorwort zu Webern's Liedern
An einen Musikkritiker
Für echt niederländische Künste (weiter
Zum Mendelssohn-Preis   (hinten 2. Blatt)
Casella's Musik
An einen "Freund"
12-Tonschrift
Aphorismus: Teilnahmslosigkeit
1. Versuch zu "Neuer Klassizismus"
Fragen v. Jens Qu. — Der D i r i g e n t
Mendelssohn[-]Preis

[2]
Aphorisms (2)
Die heutige Jugend (1)
Louis ist Kritiker
Die Kultur hat die Tendenz (1)
Vortrag: Breslau, Glückl. Hand (3)
Schutzbund f. Geistige Kultur (1)
Die mir die Nachwelt geraubt (1)
Ich habe über Gustav Mahler (1)
. . . gewissenlose Spekulanten . . . (1)
Werke der Tonkunst werden heute mangels (1)

---

* The following three tables of contents (typed carbon copies) were included with the list. The first two belong to Manuscript List B: "Kleine Manuskripte," I and II, 29 and 30, respectively; the third apparently does not relate to any items on the list.

Addenda to Manuscript List B

a) Vorwort zu op 22, handschr (2)
b)   '' '' '' '' ''   maschin (6)
Ich sehe mit Schrecken, dass Sevcik (1)

[3]
Fragments:

Outline of a theory of c o u n t e r p. ⟋carbon copy⟋
   '' '' ''   '' '' Satzkunst (Instrumen-
   (manuscr)   tations lehre []]

5 single sheets
a) Unrecht eines Künstlers
b) Zusammenhang (carbon copy)
c) d) e) Gesetze, Regeln, Lehrsätze, Definitionen

Appendix IV

Index of Aphorisms

Index of Aphorisms

Index of Aphorisms

Index of Aphorisms

Index of Aphorisms

Index of Aphorisms

---

* Schoenberg's "answer" is a watercolor.

Index of Aphorisms

Index of Aphorisms

Index of Aphorisms

*I*ndex of *A*phorisms

List of References

Bailey, Walter B. "Schoenberg's Published Articles: A List of Titles, Sources and Translations." *Journal of the Arnold Schoenberg Institute* 4, no. 2 (November 1980): 155-91.

Christensen, Jean. "Arnold Schoenberg's Oratorio *Die Jakobsleiter.*" 2 vols. Ph.D. dissertation, University of California, Los Angeles, 1979.

──────── . "Developing the Good Instincts of the Public: Schoenberg as Advocate of the Arts." *Sinfonian* 32, no. 3 (Spring 1983): 6.

──────── . "The Spiritual and the Material in Schoenberg's Thinking." *Music and Letters* 65, no. 4 (October 1984): 337-44.

Freitag, Eberhard. *Arnold Schönberg in Selbstzeugnissen und Bilddokumenten.* Reinek/Hamburg: Rowohlt Taschenbuch Verlag, 1973.

Konzert-Kalender 1911/12. Konzert-Taschenbuch für die Saison 4. Munich: Konzert-Bureau Emil Gutmann, 1911.   **Gutmanns Konzert-Kalender 1911/12**

Maegaard, Jan. *Studien zur Entwicklung des dodekaphonen Satzes bei Arnold Schönberg.* 3 vols. Copenhagen: Edition Wilhelm Hansen, 1972.

Op de Coul, Paul, and Rutger Schonte. "Schoenberg in the Netherlands." *Journal of the Arnold Schoenberg Institute* 6, no. 2 (November 1982): 141-74.

Reich, Willi. *Schoenberg: A Critical Biography.* Translated by Leo Black. London: Longman Group, 1971.

Ringer, Alexander. "Faith and Symbol—On Arnold Schoenberg's Last Musical Utterance." *Journal of the Arnold Schoenberg Institute* 6, no. 1 (June 1982): 80-95.

Rognoni, Luigi. *Espressionismo e dodecafonia.* Turin: Einaudi Editore, 1954.

Rufer, Josef. *The Works of Arnold Schoenberg: A Catalog of His Compositions, Writings and Paintings.* Translated by Dika Newlin. New York: Free Press of Glencoe, 1963.

Gedenkaus-   Schoenberg, Arnold. *Gedenkausstellung 1974.* Edited by Ernst Hilmar.
stellung **1974**   Vienna: Universal Edition, 1974.

"Gedruckte   ——— · "Gedruckte Artikel, Aphorismen, Etc." Schoenberg's un-
Artikel"   published list of published materials, deposited in the Archives of the Arnold Schoenberg Institute.

30 Kanons   ——— · *30 Kanons.* Edited by Joseph Rufer. Kassel: Bärenreiter, 1963.

——— · *Letters.* Edited by Erwin Stein. Translated by Eithne Wilkins and Ernst Kaiser. London: Faber and Faber, 1975.

——— · [List of Categories.] Schoenberg's unpublished list of his classifications for use in his catalog system. In the Archives of the Arnold Schoenberg Institute. Transcribed in Appendix I.

Ms. List A   ——— · "List of Manuscripts." Schoenberg's unpublished list of his personal papers. In the Archives of the Arnold Schoenberg Institute. Transcribed in Appendix II.

Ms. List B   ——— · "List of manuscripts of articles, essays, sketches, etc." Schoenberg's list of his papers. In the Archives of the Arnold Schoenberg Institute. Transcribed in Appendix III.

——— · *Sämtliche Werke.* Edited by Josef Rufer, et al. Mainz: Schott; Vienna: Universal Edition, 1966- .

——— · *Schöpferische Konfessionen.* Edited by Willi Reich. Zurich: Verlag der Arche, 1964.

Vojtech,   ——— · *Stil und Gedanke: Aufsätze zur Musik.* Vol. 1, *Gesammelte*
Schriften   *Schriften.* Edited by Ivan Vojtech. Reutlingen: Fischer, 1976.

SI 50   ——— · *Style and Idea.* New York: Philosophical Library, 1950.

————— · *Style and Idea.* Edited by Leonard Stein. Translated by Leo   *SI 75*
Black. London: Faber and Faber, 1975.

————— · *Texte: Die glückliche Hand, Totentanz der Prinzipien, Requiem,*
Die Jakobsleiter. Vienna: Universal Edition, 1926.

Spies, Claudio. "'Vortrag / 12 K / Princeton.'" *Perspectives of New Music*
13, no. 1 (Fall-Winter 1974): 58-136.

Steuermann, Clara. "Schoenberg at Play." *Journal of the Arnold Schoenberg*
Institute 2, no. 3 (June 1978): 240-51.

Stuckenschmidt, H. H. *Arnold Schoenberg: His Life, World and Work.*
Translated by Humphrey Searle. London: John Calder, 1977.

Türcke, Berthold. "Mahler Society: A Project of Schoenberg and
Mengelberg." *Journal of the Arnold Schoenberg Institute* 7, no. 1 (June
1983): 29-92.

General Index

Numbers in italics refer to pages in the introductory essay.

Ratz, Erwin, Bio. II, 2 d

Redlich, H. F., Glossen 1

Reger, Max, Aph. I, 20.1

Reichenbach, Dr. [?], Nb. II, f

Repetition/variation in art, Frag. III, 1

Rhythm, Frag. III, 1; Frag. VI, 1; Aph. I, 49 e; Nb. IV, a

Riemann, Hugo, Bio. V, 1; Aph. II, 1

Rubsamen, Walter, Bio. II, 2 i

Rufer, Josef, *6n, 8, 14*; Bio. II, 2 d; Bio. III, 42; Frag. V, 9

Schacht, Peter, Kl. Ms. I, 8

Schalk, Franz, Kl. Ms. III, 3

Scheinpflug, Paul, Bio. III, 22

Schilling, Max von, Bio. III, 33

Schnabel, Artur, Bio. III, 48

Schoenberg, Arnold

    ANEKDOTEN: *6*

    anti-elitism: Bio. III, 33; Kl. Ms. I, 13; Kl. Ms. II, 8; Aph. I, 9, 35

    APHORISMEN: *7, 8n, 9, 10, 11, 12*

    aphorisms: *14*

    artistic intentions/process: Bio. I, 1; Bio. III, 16, 18, 19, 22, 39, 50; Bio. IV, 1; Frag. I, 2, 3; Frag. IV, 6; Dich. 4 a, p; Aph. I, 24 f, 31, 49 c, d; Nb. II, n, d; Nb. III c

    audiences (relationship to): Bio. III, 25, 32, 43, 44; Frag. VI, 4; Aph. I, 25 f, 49 h

    autobiography (planned): *9-10*; Bio. II, 1-2; Bio. III, 7; Frag. VI, 3

    BIOGRAPHISCHES: *6n, 7, 9, 11, 12, 14*

    biography: (early life) Bio. III, 35; Bio. V, 1; (family) Bio. II, 2 g; Bio. III, 5, 10; Nb. II, e, k; (military service) Bio. V, 1; Dich. 4 x, z, gg; Aph. I, 14, 24 b, d; (emigration) Bio. III, 47, 48; (50-year celebration) Bio. III, 9; (75-year celebration) Frag. V, 6; (health) Bio. V, 8.1, 8.2-3; Aph. I, 9a; (finances) Bio. III, 31, 38, 47, 49; Frag. I, 8; Aph. I, 54; Nb. II, t, r; Orch. II, 2 b; (colleagues/publishers) Bio. III, 13, 15, 17, 22, 29, 30, 31, 33, 39, 41; (composing) Bio. III, 16, 18, 19, 46, 50; Bio. IV, 1; (performances/royalties) Bio. III, 4, 8, 14, 20, 21, 42, 43, 44, 47; Frag. V, 4, 6, 9; Orch. I, 5, 8, 10; (organizations) Bio. III, 21, 34; Kl. Ms. II, 8; Kl. Ms. III, 3, 10; (details of professional life) Bio. III, 48, 49; (résumés) Bio. V, 2-8; (dictionary entries) Bio. I, 1, 2

    development/influences: Bio. II, 1, 2; Bio. III, 17, 29, 41; Dich. 4 p, x, bb, ff; Aph. I, 16, 18, 24 b, 25 e, 26 a, 28, 30 a, 32, 45

    DICHTUNGEN: *5*

Schoenberg, Arnold (*continued*)

  doodles: Bio. III, 15, 48; Frag. V, 2, 3; Frag. VI, 4; Kl. Ms. I, 15; Kl. Ms. II, 9; Kl. Ms. III, 2 c; Aph. I, 60 a; Glossen 2; Nb. II, u

  enemies/opponents: Bio. II, 2 a, i, k; Bio. III, 30, 31, 32, 50; Frag. IV, 4; Kl. Ms. I, 3; Kl. Ms. II, g; Dich. 4 y, bb; Aph. I, 24 c, 28

  followers/imitators: Bio. III, 15, 30; Frag. IV, 9; Dich. 4 e, o, q, s, dd; Aph. I, 4, 17, 24 g, 26 a, 30 b, 39, 46 d, 48; Aph. II, 2 d

  FRAGMENTE: *6,* 6n

  games/toys/jokes: (*vexier etui*) *9*; Bio. III, 45.1, 45.2; Frag. VI, 5; Kl. Ms. I, 9, 11; Kl. Ms. II, 9; Kl. Ms. III, 3; Dich. 4 w, ee; Aph. I, 10, 17, 24 e, 44, 54

  Jens Quer. (Schoenberg's alter ego): Bio. III, 24, 26; Kl. Ms. I, 15; Aph. I, 20.2; J.Q. 1-6

  JENS QUER (category): *12*

  JEW: *6*

  KLEINE MANUSKRIPTE: *6, 8n, 11*

  letters to Schoenberg: (from Goedemanns) Kl. Ms. I, 6; (from Schünemann) Kl. Ms. I, 7; (from Buchenan) Aph. I, 51

  letters from Schoenberg (all drafts): (to Int. Soc. New Music) Bio. III, 21; (to Director, U. E.) Bio. III, 22; (to Jens. Quer.) Bio. III, 26; (to Zemlinsky) Bio. III, 27; (to Mengelberg) Bio. III, 34; (to E. Stein or Rufer) Bio. III, 42; (circular letter) Bio. III, 47; (telegram to Schnabel) Bio. III, 48; (to Von Klein Smid) Bio. III, 49; (to military authorities of Austro-Hungarian government) Bio. V, 1; (to unidentified person) Bio. V, 8; (to American conductors) Frag. V, 6; (to Kroll-Oper, Berlin) Frag. V, 9; (to unidentified supporters) Frag. VI, 4; (to unidentified journal) Kl. Ms. I, 3; (unidentified addressee) Kl. Ms. I, 12; (unidentified) Kl. Ms. I, 12; (unidentified) Kl. Ms. I, 13; (formal thank-you letter) Kl. Ms. II, 6; (to Viennese newspaper) Kl. Ms. II, 11; (to Furtwängler) Kl. Ms. III, 10; (to *The Etude*) Aph. I, 5; (circular thank-you letter) Aph. I, 16; (by Hoffman, AS' assistant, to American composers) Orch. I, 8, 9

  lists (Schoenberg's): "List of Categories" (transcribed in Appendix I) *6n, 13;* "List of Manuscripts" ("Manuscript List A," transcribed in Appendix II) *5, 6, 6n, 7, 12, 14;* "Gedruckte Artikel, Aphorismen, etc." *5, 5n;* "List of Manuscripts of articles, essays, sketches, etc." ("Manuscript List B," transcribed in Appendix III) *6, 14;* "Notes and Indexes" *6, 6n*

  literary practices: ("Abschrift") *7;* (binding) *3;* (concept papers) *3;* (copies) *12;* (dating) *13;* (grammar/spelling) *11, 12;* (organization of papers) *6-8*

  MISCELLANEOUS: *12*

  MORAL: *6*

  MUSIKALISCHES: *7, 12*

  NATUR: *6*

Schoenberg, Arnold (*continued*)

NOTEBOOKS: *11, 12*

moral concepts: Frag. IV, 2; Kl. Ms. III, 2 a-c; Aph. I, 40, 41, 42; Aph. II, 2 e, 6; Nb. I, j; Orch. II, 2 a

painting/drawing: Bio. III, 12, 29; Aph. I, 51; Nb. II, s; Nb. V, b

penmanship/signature: Bio. III, 1; Frag. VI, 5; Nb. II, u

philosophy: Kl. Ms. III, 2 a-c; Dich. 4 t; Aph. I, 2, 34, 59; Aph. II, 2 c; Nb. III, c

religious faith/beliefs: Frag. II, 2; Aph. II, 6; Nb. I, j; Orch. II, 2 a

reputation: Bio. III, 25, 30, 37, 50; Bio. V, 1; Frag. IV, 4; Kl. Ms. II, 9, 11; Dich. 4 w; Aph. I, 24 a, 52

self-evaluation: Bio. I, 1; Bio. III, 2; Bio. III, 9, 12, 17, 18, 19, 29; Dich. 4, a, p, bb, ff; Aph. I, 2, 9, 16, 19, 24 f, g, 25 g, 26 h, 30 a, 32

social/politicial concepts: Bio. III, 32, 33; Kl. Ms. III, 3; Aph. I, 3 c, 9, 25 c, i, 58; Aph. II, 5 a, b, 7, 9 b

speeches/lectures: (announcement for lecture) Bio. III, 38; (on art evaluation) Frag. III, 2; (draft) Aph. V, 7; (*Glückliche Hand*) Kl. Ms. II, 6, 7; (Princeton lecture) Kl. Ms. III, 8

supernatural phenomena/premonitions: Bio. III, 16, 20; Kl. Ms. III, 3; Dich. 4 l, v; Aph. I, 25 e, 46 e, 49 a; An. 1, 2

teaching: Bio. III, 3, 36, 37, 38; Frag. I, 8; Kl. Ms. I, 8; Kl. Ms. III, 13; Orch. I-III

thumbprints: Bio. III, 1; Aph. I, 2, 3, 4, 5, 6, 8; J.Q. 3

works:

a) musical compositions

Bach Chorale Prelude, Bio. III, 31; *Das Buch der hängenden Gärten,* op. 15, Bio. III, 50; Canons, Kl. Ms. I, 1, 5; Kl. Ms. III, 1; (texts) Kl. Ms. III, 9; Dich. 6; *Chamber Symphony,* op. 9, Bio. III, 11, 39, 42, 43; (internal logic) Frag. V, 7; Concertgebouw canon, Kl. Ms. I, 1; (sketch for dedication) Kl. Ms. I, 5; I, 6; Kl. Ms. III, 9; *Drei Satiren,* op. 28, Bio. III, 46; Kl. Ms. I, 14; Dich. 5.1-.4; *Erwartung,* op. 17, Bio. III, 19; *Four Orchestra Songs,* op. 22 (drafts for preface), Kl. Ms. II, 13, 14; *Four Pieces for Mixed Chorus,* op. 27, (texts) Dich. 5.1-.4; *Die glückliche Hand,* op. 18, (draft for lecture on) Kl. Ms. II, 6, 7; *Gurre-Lieder,* 6n; Bio. III, 8, 19, 22, 31, 50; Kl. Ms. III, 3, 8; Aph. II, 2 e; "Hans im Glück" (draft) Frag. I, 6; *Die Jakobsleiter,* Bio. III, 19, 23; (newspaper report) Bio. III, 27; Aph. I, 51, 60 b; *Moses und Aron,* Bio. IV, 1; *Der neue Klassizismus* (draft of text), Kl. Ms. I, 14; *Pelleas und Melisande,* op. 5, Bio. III, 11, 42; (program) Frag. I, 7; *Piano Pieces,* op. 11, Bio. III, 50; *Pierrot Lunaire,* op. 12, Bio. III, 19; (Puccini's interest) Bio. III, 28; *Serenade,* op. 24, Kl. Ms. II, 15; *Six Pieces for Male Chorus,* op. 35, Dich. 3; *Songs,* op. 1, no. 2, Bio. III, 11; op. 2, Bio. III, 50; op. 3, no. 3, Bio. III, 11; op. 6, Bio. III, 50; *String Quartet* No. 2, op. 10, Bio. III, 14, 19, 42; No. 3, op. 30, Bio. III, 19; *Suite,* op. 29, Bio. III, 27; *A Survivor From Warsaw,* op. 46, Dich. 1, 5; Nb. II, i; *Variations for Orchestra,*

About the Authors

JEAN CHRISTENSEN, associate professor of music history at the University of Louisville, wrote her dissertation "Arnold Schoenberg's Oratorio, Die Jakobsleiter" *(University of California, Los Angeles, 1979) with the assistance of a George C. Marshall Fellowship and a Martha Baird Rockefeller Award in Musicology. Further studies of Schoenberg and Per Nørgård (b. 1932) have been supported by grants from the American-Scandinavian Foundation, the National Endowment for the Humanities, the American Philosophical Society, and the University of Louisville. She has written articles and reviews for* Arts and Letters, Journal of the Arnold Schoenberg Institute, Musical Quarterly, *and* Notes.

Collaboration with JESPER CHRISTENSEN began in the area of 20th-century Danish music. The authors are presently preparing an annotated bibliography of Arnold Schoenberg.